ICONS OF THE MAHABHARATA

Undefeatable KRISHNA

ICONS OF THE MAHABHARATA

Undefeatable KRISHNA

The Supreme Strategist's Timeless Wisdom for Navigating Modern Life

SHUBHA VILAS

JAICO PUBLISHING HOUSE

Ahmedabad Bangalore Chennai
Delhi Hyderabad Kolkata Mumbai

Published by Jaico Publishing House
A-2 Jash Chambers, 7-A Sir Phirozshah Mehta Road
Fort, Mumbai - 400 001
jaicopub@jaicobooks.com
www.jaicobooks.com

ICONS OF THE MAHABHARATA
Undefeatable Krishna – Book 1
ISBN 978-93-49358-17-1

First Jaico Impression: 2025

Page design and layout by R. Ajith Kumar, Delhi

Printed by
Thomson Press India Limited, New Delhi

यतो धर्मस्ततः कृष्णो यतः कृष्णस्ततो जयः ।
यतः कृष्णस्ततो धर्मो यतो धर्मस्ततो जयः ।

Yato dharmastatah krishno yatah krishnastato jayah
Mahabharata 6.41.55

Yatah krishnastato dharmo yato dharmastato jayah
Mahabharata 13.153.39

"Where there is righteousness, there is Krishna.
Where there is Krishna, success follows.
Where there is Krishna, righteousness prevails.
Where there is righteousness, victory is assured."

CONTENTS

INTRODUCTION

The *Mahabharata* is an ocean—deep, vast, and unfathomable. Only an expert diver can uncover hidden treasures from its depths. I do not claim to be an expert as I embark on this monumental journey of writing a series of books on the *Mahabharata*. I am but an eager student, captivated by its profundities and mysteries. My courage to dive deep into this sacred epic comes solely from the blessings of my gurus, mentors, and teachers. As I venture into the many unknowns, I offer my respects to Sage Vyasa—the divine architect of wisdom, the sage who saw, compiled, and gifted the world the *Mahabharata*, the essence of all knowledge.

This is my second major literary expedition after *Ramayana: The Game of Life*—a six-volume series on the *Ramayana* through the lens of life lessons. The overwhelming love and encouragement from thousands of readers—curious seekers and seasoned spiritualists alike—has emboldened me to explore the *Mahabharata*. The *Ramayana* series had taken a decade of intense study. At more than four times the length, the *Mahabharata* demands an even deeper and more expansive exploration.

The *Mahabharata* is more than just a story about kings and wars. It is the mirror of life that reflects the deepest truths of human nature, destiny, and dharma. Nowhere is this more evident than in the life and actions of Krishna, who moves through the epic not just as a warrior or a diplomat, but as the very voice of divine wisdom guiding the course of history.

The *Mahabharata* is more than just an epic. It is a vast repository of wisdom waiting to be explored and shared with the world. This 'encyclopedia of human existence' captures the entire spectrum of emotions, dilemmas, and philosophies that shape life. The verse *"Yad ihaasti tad anyatra, yan nehaasti na tat kvachit"* (Mahabharata 1.56.33) means "Whatever is found here can be found elsewhere, but what is not found here cannot be found anywhere". This alone outlines the sheer magnitude of the *Mahabharata*, making it a timeless guide for all aspects of life.

Ramayana: The Game of Life followed a structured, linear retelling of the epic, but my approach to the *Mahabharata* is markedly different. I call it 'story analytics'—a fusion of immersive storytelling and sharp character analyses unfolding in a non-linear, non-chronological fashion. The first step toward realizing this vision is *Icons of the Mahabharata*—a multi-volume series centered on key personalities from this magnificent epic. This series goes beyond a mere retelling; it is an expedition into this ocean of existence through the lives of these extraordinary personalities. I aim to uncover different layers of these characters—their choices, challenges, dilemmas, strengths, virtues, and flaws—to present you with the timeless relevance of their stories and offer a fresh perspective on these legendary figures. The analyses will be sharp, but the heart of the books will remain the stories—vivid, poignant, and timeless.

This is only the beginning. The *Mahabharata* cannot be confined to a single series. Over time, I envision multiple explorations—series and standalone works—to illuminate its wisdom in ways yet undiscovered. Only time will tell where this journey leads. But now, let us first plunge into this infinite ocean with *Icons of the Mahabharata.*

Each book in the *Icons of the Mahabharata* series promises to replicate the journey of a river from its humble origins to its mighty confluence with the ocean.

Section one—like the river's source—will trace each character's stories, trials, choices, and life lessons from their journeys. Let these flow through you, as a river courses through mountains and valleys, and shape your understanding of life.

Section two—like the river's confluence with the ocean—will merge each character's experiences with timeless wisdom. Explore the teachings and philosophies imparted by the character and apply these to navigate life's biggest challenges, much like a river overcomes endless obstacles before surrendering to the infinite embrace of the ocean.

The first in this series is *Undefeatable Krishna* which presents Lord Krishna in a manner not attempted before. He is the heartbeat of the *Mahabharata*—an enigmatic and endearing figure whose presence shapes the destiny of all crossing his path. This book dives deep into his multifaceted persona—his boundless love, unshakable wisdom, unmatched strategic acumen, and unwavering compassion.

The first section recounts Krishna's actions and analyses his role as the ultimate problem-solver, the ever-watchful guide, and the infallible force behind the epic's unfolding events. Each chapter uncovers a unique aspect of Krishna, revealing how his divine qualities remain relevant even today. *Undefeatable Krishna* is the *Mahabharata* seen through the eyes of its most pivotal character—the one who remains undefeated not just in battle but in the hearts of those who seek truth and wisdom.

The second section explains relevant verses from the *Bhagavad Gita* vis-à-vis the pressing challenges of our times—uncertainty, stress, and moral dilemmas. In such a world, the wisdom of Krishna remains as relevant as ever. Imagine sitting across from Krishna and asking him the most soul-stirring questions about purpose, fear, relationships, success, failure, and inner peace. What would he say? How would he guide you? This section explores nine of the most critical challenges humans face today through real-life case studies and finds practical solutions from Krishna's timeless teachings in the *Bhagavad Gita*.

Undefeatable Krishna is an actionable guide to navigating life's greatest struggles with clarity, confidence, and conviction. Whether you seek strength in adversity, wisdom in decision-making, or peace in chaos, Krishna's voice will act as the life-transforming masterclass in living, thinking, and thriving in the world today. To make the most of this book, flow with it, read at your own pace, pause to reflect, and most importantly, let Krishna's wisdom become a part of your journey.

If this book (and series) makes you joyful, inspires you, deepens your faith, brings you more clarity, or evokes any other emotion in you, kindly stop for a moment and offer a small prayer so that I may be able to find the intelligence and ability to present the *Mahabharata* in a way that impacts humanity for decades.

I

1

ARE YOU READY?

2.22.13

यस्यां यस्यामवस्थायां यद्यत्कर्म करोति यः ।
तस्यां तस्यामवस्थायां तत्फलं समवाप्नुयात् ॥

Yasyaam yasyaamavasthaayaam yadyatkarma karoti yah
Tasyaam tasyaamavasthaayaam tatphalam samavaapnuyaat

"Whatever actions one takes in any circumstance, they must experience the results of those actions in that state of being."

Whatever happened, happened for the good; what is happening is happening for the good; whatever will happen will also happen for the good.

Unequal Half

War. They were always at odds from the moment they became aware of each other's existence. The five Pandavas and the hundred Kauravas shared nothing but relentless envy, deep hatred, bitter rivalry, and constant unease. *How do we destroy them?* Time pushed them so far apart that plotting to eliminate the adversary became an everyday thing. Murder was always lurking.

Duryodhana's several attempts to kill the Pandavas became so frequent and ruthless that Bhishma, the family elder, felt compelled to suggest a way out to Dhritarashtra. "You and Pandu were both precious to me. So are your sons. I cannot approve of this savage animosity. Make peace with the Pandavas. Give them half the land." Turning to Duryodhana he said, "You feel entitled to this kingdom, so do the Pandavas. You may have begun to believe that this kingdom is rightfully yours. They think the same, too, because their father ruled this land before your father did. So, settle this dispute; give them what is theirs—half the kingdom. It will be best for everyone. If you decide otherwise, it could be the worst decision yet."

Dronacharya agreed with Bhishma, as did Vidura. So, when the Pandavas returned with Draupadi, Dhritarashtra said to Yudhishthira, "I give you and your brothers Khandavaprastha to end this contention between you and your cousins. Take that half and set up your kingdom there. No one will try to harm you."

The kingdom was halved, but the division was far from equal. Dhritarashtra gave his sons the capital and the best half of the kingdom. He gave the Pandavas the barren and remote half. The Pandavas knew of the division disparity and the worthlessness of their half of the land. Yet, they gladly accepted the offer. With Krishna by their side, the Pandavas, Draupadi, and Kunti, headed out to Khandavaprastha. *We will make the best of what we have.*

Treating symptoms rather than the underlying cause exacerbates the problem.[1]

One steamy summer's day, Arjuna went up to Krishna. "This scorching heat is unbearable. Let us go to the banks of the Yamuna—the only spot of relief in this severe weather. We could spend all day there and return in the evening."

"I wish the same. Let us go and relax with our family and friends."

The two friends took Yudhishthir's permission to head off to the perfect spot full of tall trees by the Yamuna and set up a camp. When everyone was busy doing their own thing—dancing, singing, or spending quality time in their tents—Krishna and Arjuna went for a stroll. They reached a rock not far from where the others were. Sitting on the rock, their feet caressing the refreshing waters, the two friends began sharing memories and stories of victories and talking about this and that.

True friendship offers an unconditional presence in times of crisis.

---

1 Offering the barren half of the kingdom was a fake move to pacify them. The intent was never to root out the dispute; it was more a token cover-up gesture for all the harm the Kauravas inflicted on the Pandavas. The property partition was more of a stopgap measure than a long-term remedy for their problems.

Fire and Water

They were deep in conversation when an old, tall brahman with unique, arresting features approached them. Arjuna stared at the brahman, his mouth agape and palms unconsciously folded in reverence. He had never seen anyone as radiant before. His matted locks, ragged clothes, sunshine yellow beard with a hint of green, eyes like lotus petals, and a complexion so bright that Arjuna could not fathom the incredible energy that seemed just waiting to be unleashed from that feeble body. Both Krishna and Arjuna stood up to welcome the mysterious brahman.

"I am hungry!" The old sage's voice sizzled. "I am ravenously hungry, but I have been denied food. Can the two of you help satisfy my hunger by bringing me enough food?

Intrigued by the unusual request, Krishna and Arjuna wanted to know more. "What kind of food do you want? We are more than happy to feed you to your heart's desire."

"I am not looking for any ordinary food. I am Agni, the fire deity with an endless appetite. I wish to eat this entire Khandava forest to satisfy my appetite. The only hitch is Indra will not let me. His friend Naga Takshaka lives here with his family and followers. Indra is extremely cautious about the forest and refuses to let me touch it because of his promise to protect Takshaka forever. Each time I start a forest fire somewhere to consume it, Indra's clouds douse it. I am craving the Khandava forest. You are good with weapons. So please stop Indra from raining on me whenever I try to consume Khandava," Agni pleaded.

Agni wanted Krishna and Arjuna to be completely convinced about helping him. "Here is a little story about how it came down to this. Perhaps that will help you decide. King Shvetaki liked fire sacrifices and performed them so often that the brahmans in his kingdom had had enough. He rewarded them well after each sacrifice, but the exhaustion from the labor and effort that went into performing these sacrifices was too much to bear. They felt so overworked that they stopped advising him and told him, 'You can only achieve your goals with divine intervention. Worship Lord Shiva and ask him to grant your wishes.'"

"Shvetaki spent years performing rigorous *tapasya* on Mount Kailash, until Lord Shiva appeared and asked, 'What do you want?' 'I want the gods to assist in my sacrifice.' Shiva reminded Shvetaki, 'The gods do not assist humans, but I will make an exception for you on one condition. You will have to live a life of celibacy and perform a twelve-year-long sacrifice, offering ghee to Agni. If you succeed, I will get you all the help you need.' The king followed all instructions. A dozen years later, he returned to Lord Shiva. 'I am grateful for your sacrifices. But only a brahman can help you with sacrifices. I recommend Durvasa *muni*, who is a part of me, to help you finish your sacrifices.'

Everything went fine for the king, but one entity suffered through all of this—me, Agni. For twelve straight years, I had to drink copious amounts of ghee. I am sick from all that ghee. You know that the fire in the sacred altar is my tongue. So I went from looking magnificent to deathly pale. I asked the all-knowing Brahma for advice to cure my illness. He suggested that I consume the Khandava forest, which he was certain had many medicinal herbs to cure this affliction."

There is always a dark side to success: Someone, somewhere, suffers in silence when someone, somewhere, celebrates aloud.

"No sooner than I heard it, I rushed to this forest and set it ablaze. But, in a matter of moments, Indra helped the creatures in this forest put out the fire. He did this every time I started a fire. Brahma pitied me and suggested that I visit the heavenly twins, Nara and Narayana on earth, in their current incarnation near the Khandava forest. Those twins are you! Brahma has said that you would help without a doubt. I am here because of his assurance.

It takes courage, not weakness, to ask for help, for it needs courage to admit one's weakness.

Arjuna did not hesitate to help. "But I have some conditions. I have an abundance of celestial missiles, but I need a bow capable of withstanding the ferocity and intensity of Indra's showers. I also need an endless supply of arrows. This ordinary chariot cannot accommodate all of those special weapons, so I will need to build a chariot strong enough to handle the weight. I would prefer the chariot be pulled by heavenly horses that are white as snow and swift as the wind. The chariot should be as shiny as the sun, and its wheels should rumble as thunder. Besides, it would be fitting if Krishna were given a weapon as powerful as Lord Shiva's most devastating missile."

Ready or Not?

"Considering the severity of the impending conflict, your demands are justified. Only the foolish would enter such a conflict unprepared," Agni said, agreeing to his requests. He immediately summoned Varuna, the water god, and said, "Please give me your celestial bow, the inexhaustible quiver, and the magnificent chariot given by the moon god." Varuna swiftly and magically obtained all of it. Agni took it and handed it over to Arjuna, saying, "This studded bow is the Gandiva. With this in your hand, you will be famous. Its energy is boundless, and no weapon can harm it. It is more powerful than a million bows combined. It is the crown treasure of celestial weaponry. It is as beautiful as it is functional.

Prepare before facing life's battles because being unprepared means preparing for failure.

Agni also gave Arjuna an exceptional chariot. "Here is the chariot pulled by white-as-snow ethereal horses born in the celestial realm of the Gandharvas. They gallop like the wind. The chariot is unstoppable, fearsome, and stocked with the finest tools and weapons. Nothing in the universe can damage its wheels. Its radiance rivals the sun, and its powerful roar could be heard from miles away. Prajapati created it after thousands of years of meditation and abstinence. The chariot's stunning golden flagstaff has a banner bearing the insignia of a fierce lionlike *vanara*. The gaze in the insignia can actually burn anything in its vicinity."

Arjuna approached the chariot and circumambulated it with his palms folded in reverence. He looked impressive and formidable in the golden armor and slung two sheathed swords on a golden belt. He beamed, and his confidence surged as he lifted the magnificent bow fashioned by Lord Brahma himself. He held the bow down, leaned forward, and secured the string. Arjuna felt a powerful charge run down his spine with the first twang of the Gandiva. He had never heard as commanding a reverberation before and was instantly drawn to the Gandiva. He knew it would be his companion for life.

Agni then shifted his attention to Krishna. He handed him an exquisite present—a golden disk with an iron core. "When you hurl this disk at the enemy, it becomes fiery and causes unimaginable destruction. When you wield this weapon, it will be known as the Sudarshana *chakra*. Undeniably the best weapon in all three realms, it can destroy everything in this universe—humans, deities, nagas, rakshasas, *pishacha*s, and *daitya*s. Once it destroys its target, it will return to you. It will manifest your thoughts and fulfill all of your desires." Varuna then gave Krishna a special mace. "Take this Kaumodaki *gada*. When you wield it, it will roar like thunder and shatter the hearts and limbs of your enemies."

This is the flow chart of success in a mission:
Gather purpose → people (manpower)
→ prowess (skills and authority)
→ resources(things) → recognition → gratitude.

Krishna said to Agni, "O, Exalted One! Now that we are armed and ready, we can take on Indra."

Arjuna said, "Go ahead and set ablaze the Khandava forest. You can count on us to counter every force in the three realms that tries to stop you."

Agni, motivated by these words, assumed a monstrous shape and loomed over the entire Khandava forest. He split himself into seven large columns of flames and swooped down on the forest from seven different directions. Agni's confidence soared and quickly began spreading across the forest, devouring everything. With weapons drawn and mounted on the celestial chariot, Arjuna swiftly circled the vast forest. Krishna, too, hopped onto his chariot and swirled around the forest alongside Arjuna. The speeding chariots blurred in the fiery chaos, only their rumbling noises giving away their presence.

Vibes do not lie. The vibe at the onset of a venture determines its outcome. Self-confidence empowers the vibe of victory.

Slaying Some, Saving Some

Agni's scorching waves sent the forest creatures fleeing in every direction. As the demonic creatures emerged from the forest's perimeter, Arjuna's arrows felled them. Agni began to heal as he consumed all the medicinal herbs and plants in the forest. Krishna and Arjuna monitored those escaping the periphery by land and those attempting to fly away. Arjuna's arrow would hunt down those in flight. The forest soon became a raging inferno, the massive flames playfully licking the clouds as if to taunt them.

The celestials rushed to Indra. "Agni has set the Khandava on fire again!" Indra was livid. "How dare he interfere in the territory I have marked out for my friends?"

Takshaka, a naga, had taken shelter in the Khandava forest, trusting his friend Indra. Over time, Takshaka expanded his family and army and gained control of every nook and cranny of the vast expanse, preventing any humans from ever setting foot in the forest. Because of the unusual bond they shared, Indra assured Takshaka of protection.

Arjuna was Indra's son, but his actions were now putting the promise he had made to his friend at risk. Unable to bear the insult, Indra began filling the sky with monstrous rain clouds, each big enough to flood an entire city with one cloudburst. Hundreds of thousands clouds gathered over Khandava, rumbling and roaring—as if to mock and announce the deluge of downpour. No matter how hot the flames, the raindrops doused them. Soon, the heavy showers extinguished the fire, leaving dense smoke over the forest in the aftermath.

Arjuna was all set for this moment. He quickly unleashed a barrage of arrows into the sky. Soon, the arrows interweaved into a breathtaking, imporous canopy over the forest. Although preoccupied with staving off the rain, Arjuna did not let any animal leave the forest. Arjuna continued shooting arrows with incredible speed, not missing a single target. Takshaka's son, Ashwasena, tried to flee, but Arjuna kept him trapped between the raging fire and his barrage of whizzing arrows. Ashwasena's father was not in the forest at the time, so his mother rushed to his aid. To save her son from harm, she swallowed his head and started to slide his entire body into her belly. She then soared skywards to take refuge among Indra's clouds. But just as she was about to reach the clouds, an arrow sprang out of nowhere and severed her head. As his mother fell to the ground, Ashwasena slipped out of her belly. Noticing the grave situation, Indra unleashed a raging windstorm on Arjuna, knocking him out for a split second. Ashwasena took advantage of the gap and escaped.

Focus does not guarantee absolute freedom from mistakes, but the key is maintaining unwavering resolve and attention no matter what happens.

Indra's trickery infuriated Arjuna. He directed all his fury at his father, showering arrows at him. Indra released a massive thundercloud laced with lightning to counter the arrows crowding the sky. Arjuna used only one arrow—the Vayavya *astra*—to suck the cloud dry and drain away all the thunder energy. The cloud quickly disappeared, and the sun returned. With the sun shining bright, Agni regained energy and burned more fiercely than before. Indra's state of powerlessness prompted the dwelling nagas, *daityas*, rakshasas, and *danavas* to unleash their entire barrage of magical weapons on the two friends. The battle became fiercer as Arjuna's arrows and Krishna's disk slaughtered and slashed thousands of enemies, feeding the flames. Soon, a swarm of celestial beings—Surya,

Chandra, Skanda, Mitra, and countless more—began assaulting Krishna and Arjuna with their divine weapons. The two warriors fought weapon for weapon.

The greatest battlefield is the space between the ears. Win the war in the mind first for triumph over the enemy.

No one could withstand their onslaught or match their vigor. Everyone conceded defeat and withdrew, but Indra was not ready to surrender. So, this time, he forced a very different rain on the two heroes—pelting stone. Arjuna fought stone for stone with one arrow that dispersed millions of arrows, each reducing every stone to dust. Infuriated by Arjuna's defiance, Indra hurtled a massive mountain peak at his son. Arjuna's arrow pulverized the peak; the debris scattered over the forest, crushing many creatures. The Krishna–Arjuna team was invincible as long as they worked in perfect harmony, reading each other's minds and strategizing in sync to destroy the enemy. Indra realized defeating the duo speeding across the skies in their chariots was impossible. His wrath gave way to admiration and pride. *My son is so mighty and powerful!* The skies parted for the celestials to return.

Just as sticks in a bundle are unbreakable, the team becomes unbeatable when individuals play off each other's synergies.

Surviving Flames and Fury

The silhouette made an attempt to slip away. Krishna's Sudarshana *chakra* would have hit the fugitive had he not seen him fall at Arjuna's feet. That quick reaction saved Maya, the asura, from certain death. "Do not fear!" Arjuna's response bewildered and calmed the shaken asura. Krishna lowered the fiery discus. Right at this moment, Mayasura decided to stay by Arjuna's side until Khandava was completely burned down.

A great leader is a paradox in motion—kind yet firm, modest yet resolute, restless yet patient, and controlled yet adaptable.

Only six survived the fire. Agni had consumed everything except Ashwasena, Mayasura, and four Sharangaka fledglings.

Sage Mandapala was an extreme ascetic who aspired for a seat in the heavens. But when he knocked on heaven's door after a long life of penance and austerities on earth, he was barred entry. *After everything that I have done, why not?* He was not expecting the answer to be, "You do not have a son." Mandapala was adamant about his place in heaven. *I must have the most number of progenies in the shortest time possible.* Then, an idea struck him. *Ah! Birds reproduced fast.* Mandapala used the corpse of a Sharangaka bird and married Jarita, a bird of another species, and she laid four eggs. As soon as the eggs hatched, leaving Jarita to do all the nurturing, he moved out of the house to procreate more with yet another bird, Lapita. Once when roaming the forests with Lapita, Mandapala saw Agni lurking in the Khandava forest. Sensing grave danger for his children, Mandapala rushed to Agni. "O Agni! The purifier of all sins … O wondrous lord! You learned master … you are … you have … you can …" Mandapala's stream of eulogies impressed Agni. "What can I do for you?" Immediately, Mandapala bowed with palms folded, "When you burn down this forest, O Lord, spare my children." Granting him his wish, Agni blazed on.

The flames were harsh and high. Jarita panicked. *What do I do? They will not survive this! They have not even grown wings yet!* "Mother, fly away. Save yourself. You can have more children. The family will survive if you escape." Jarita's heart hurt when she heard her fledglings. She could not leave them to die. So, she searched her surroundings for a safehouse for them. She found a mousehole near the root of a tree. "Now go inside and hide there. The raging flames will not hurt you. I promise to seal the entrance with clay to keep you safe from the fire." The fledglings were hesitant. "But Mother, we are just little balls of fur, the mouse will devour us. Death by fire is more honorable." Jarita assuaged their fears, "Do not worry! When the mouse emerged from this hole, I saw a hawk carry it away." The fledglings were still not convinced. "How can you be so sure the hawk ate it?" Jarita said, "I followed the hawk, so I am certain it ate the mouse." But the fledglings still refused. "We do not know, Mother, if it was the same mouse. It is better to be sure of death than to be unsure of life. We will stay in our nest. Please, Mother, fly away. You could always come back and get us if we are alive." Jarita flew away from the forest fire, abandoning her four sons.

Soon, Agni was blowing flames on the tree that housed the fledglings' nest. The little birds start singing praises to Agni. Agni was touched and remembered his promise to their father, Mandapala. "Fear not. Your father had requested me to spare your lives. I am impressed with your songs of praise."

Agni skipped their tree and continued devouring the rest of the forest. Mandapala and Jarita, who were hovering above, saw their nest spared in the fire. They went and rescued them. Arjuna and Krishna saw the family emerging from the forest but decided to spare their lives. *Agni wanted them saved!* After torching and turning the entire Khandava forest to ashes, Agni finally took a break. The thousands of medicinal herbs he had consumed along his fiery journey healed his stomach.

Friends in Deed

Agni walked up to Krishna and Arjuna. "Accept my deepest gratitude." Then Indra came by and said, "You were both incredible. I grant you both a boon of your choice. Tell me what you want." Arjuna said, "Please grant me access to all heavenly weapons at the right time." Indra agreed right away. "The moment you earn Shiva's approval, you will have unlocked access to all my celestial weapons, particularly the ones with fire and wind." Turning to Krishna, he asked, "What do you want?"

"Eternal friendship with Arjuna."

Krishna's request left Arjuna in tears. *So selfless of him! He could have asked Indra for anything and everything. Yet he has chosen eternal friendship with me. I feel so small in front of his gesture. I resolve to put my relationship with Krishna above everything else. He is the most important thing in my life.*

The greatest gift a friend can give is friendship.

The flames in Khandava forest raged unabated for fifteen days. The two friends had helped Agni without a break. Once Agni and Indra left after bestowing their boons on Krishna and Arjuna, the duo returned to the picnic spot where it all began. They picked up the strings of conversation from where they had left off. They wanted to spend some quality time together, but someone interrupted it. Mayasura understood he was unwelcome, but he felt obligated to return the favor. "O son of Kunti, your mercy spared me from the fury of Krishna and Agni. For this, I am eternally grateful. As a gesture of gratitude, I want to do something for you." Arjuna said, "O great asura, do not bother. I need nothing in exchange for rescuing your life. Let us be eternal well-wishers then. Go, live as you like. Be happy."

A bad day can become a pleasant memory when someone's kindness touches it. Gratitude is the best way to repay a favor.

Hall of Illusions

But Mayasura insisted. "I know you wish me well. But I do want to do something for you. I am an architect—the Vishwakarma of *danavas*. Please allow me to do something for you." Arjuna paused to consider his request. "If I were to ask for a favor after rescuing you from imminent death, the act of kindness would turn into a transaction. I really do not want anything from you. Nevertheless, since you are so persistent, I cannot refuse you either. Do something for Krishna, instead. I will consider that as enough recompensation from you."

Mayasura turned to Krishna. "Maya, son of Diti, if you really want to help me, build an enormous assembly hall for Yudhishthir, unmatched in splendor anywhere in the universe. Create something so remarkable that it cannot be replicated. Incorporate the architectural expertise from across the realms of the devas, asuras, and *manavas*. This is my wish."

A wide grin spread across Mayasura's face. "Of course!" He started planning right away. Arjuna and Krishna introduced him to Yudhishthir. Mayasura quickly identified a barren five-thousand-cubit-square plot and began constructing the hall of illusions. He kept his promise to Krishna and erected a magical hall for Yudhishthir. As they beheld the result of their generosity, Krishna and Arjuna could not help but smile.

Khandavaprastha was renamed Indraprastha—a once-barren plot of land had transformed into the most remarkable city.

A blessing lies within every curse.

Today's Test, Tomorrow's Testimony

The Khandavaprastha incident was a test of Arjuna's faith and trust in Krishna and his preparedness for the war ahead. The fire tested not only Arjuna's skills with weapons but also his ability to take charge and find solutions when surrounded by chaos. The heavenly beings put Arjuna through many tests to assess if he was ready to lead the army in battle against Duryodhana's adharmic forces.

Krishna made some astute observations about Arjuna during the fire that convinced him of his friend's purpose for the war.

Preparedness: Even agreeing to take up the herculean task, Arjuna was extremely focussed on preparing for it.

Perfection: Arjuna followed the greatness flowchart to perfection.

Power vibes: Arjuna's persona had begun to give off superhuman vibes—the kind that assures victory.

Focus: Arjuna's focus through the burning of Khandavaprastha remained intact. Only in one instance did Arjuna lose a target, that, too, because Indra tricked him. Yet, he recovered quickly and was back in action with greater determination.

Fearlessness: Arjuna showed no fear of even the most formidable of enemies. Outside forces could not harm him because he had won the battle in his mind.

Teamwork: Arjuna used all his strength, but he also combined it with Krishna's strength. He leveraged teamwork to gain victory.

Self-awareness: Arjuna knew when to be nice and when to be harsh. He was humble, even though he was fiercely independent. He was passionate, but he knew how to stay calm. His self-knowledge helped him channel his energies appropriately and become adept at flexible decision-making. A test aims to highlight our strengths, not our shortcomings, to encourage, not discourage, and to determine if one is prepared to take on more responsibility.

2

THE LORD OF LOVE

14.113.18

स्थावरे जङ्गमे वाऽपि सर्वभूतेषु पाण्डव ।
समत्वेन यदा कुर्यान्मद्भक्तो मित्रशत्रुषु ॥

Sthaavare jangame vaapi sarvabhooteshu paandava
Samatvena yadaa kuryaanmadbhakto mitrashatrushu

"O Pandava! A true devotee sees all beings—whether still or moving, friend or foe—with equal vision."

Love manifests from the essence of who you are. When love consumes you and fills up within you, its effervescence permeates your thoughts, words, and actions. When love is at the core of your existence, your thoughts ooze compassion, your words radiate warmth, and your actions offer comfort.

Head Over Heels

Arjuna had not even seen her, but he was already head over heels in love. Subhadra was an absolute picture-perfect dream of a woman. He had woven together this image of a stunning personality from every yarn his friend, Gada, had spun about her. Arjuna had met Krishna's cousin, Gada, at the hermitage and the two had struck up a close friendship. Back then, Gada would tell him fascinating things about his cousin Subhadra, but Arjuna never really had the chance to see her or drop by her splendid city, Dwaraka.

Sometimes, luck comes disguised as misfortune. Arjuna's voluntary dozen-year exile was one such stroke of luck. The Pandavas had vowed to each spend an entire year with Draupadi. If another Pandava brother entered Draupadi's chamber during that period, he would have to go on a voluntary dozen-year exile as penance for breaking the vow.

One day, a brahman approached Arjuna for help; someone had stolen his cows and wanted them retrieved. Arjuna was about to venture out on this new mission when he realized his bow was in Draupadi's chamber. But this was Yudhishthir's year with her. Although torn between his duty to protect and his vow to abstain, Arjuna chose duty, knowing that the discomfort would last only the next twelve years.

Through these grueling dozen years, Arjuna traveled to several places of pilgrimage, but his heart kept returning to Dwaraka, particularly to that damsel. He often felt that it would not hurt and that it would be perfectly alright to steal a glance at his dream woman when he had the chance—even if it was from a distance.

Most people let calamity trigger fears in their minds; only a few allow it to stir up dreams in their hearts.

Venturing into Dwaraka was not going to be easy—that too, without revealing his identity. After confirming that Subhadra would be in Dwaraka during the time of his visit, Arjuna reached Prabhaskshetra, a holy locality near Dwaraka.

Not long after, people noticed a very stoic-looking sannyasi meditating under a tree. Dressed in mendicant robes, *trishul* in hand, broad triple-line ash stripes across his forehead and several parts of his torso and arms, sacred Rudraksha beads around his neck, and a heap of matted hair towering over his head, the mendicant's aura was impressive. He was austerity and intense devotion personified.

Whenever Arjuna shut his eyes tight to meditate, usually, unwavering thoughts of Krishna twirled inside his head like the dancing waters of a live stream, but today was different. The disguised sannyasi's mind was a bit of a mess. Frolicking among those now-not-so-unwavering thoughts of Krishna was the smiling face of Subhadra.

The moment Arjuna began to pray fervently to Krishna for help, a sudden downpour drenched him in a flood of emotions.

Every emotion coursing through a human heart is valid and important in shaping and coloring the rainbow of life.

"Ha! Ha! Ha! Ha!"

Krishna's sudden hysterical laugh startled his wife, Satyabhama. She had not ever seen Krishna in this mood. He was not just laughing. He was cackling and holding his aching stomach, his eyes tearing up. She was curious about what triggered such a reaction. Catching his breath, Krishna said, "Ha! Ha! Ha! Cousin Arjuna's mind ... the thing running through his head right now .... Ha! Ha! Ha! Ha! Arjuna has just entered Prabhas disguised as a sannyasi and is seated under a tree, drenched in the rain! He has only one burning thought now. That thought is not about me! Ha! Ha! Ha!"

His cousin's love-sickness tickled Krishna no end. He immediately stood up to go and meet Arjuna. Satyabhama knew right away this was confidential without Krishna explicitly telling her to keep it that way.

Where there is love, there is implicit trust and confidentiality.

"So, traveling to so many holy places changed your heart after all! So much that you have decided to renounce the world at the end of your journey?" Krishna walked up to the eyes-still-shut Arjuna—a naughty smile plastered across his face. He knew his dearest friend and cousin's heart quite well, but he just wanted to have some fun at his expense. Krishna had pierced through the torrential rain in his chariot to reach Prabhas, but it did not really take him much time to find the largest banyan tree under which Arjuna sat completely wet. It had been a while since the two met. For the last twelve years, Arjuna had been traveling far and wide, and Krishna had been busy managing Dwaraka.

The moment Arjuna heard the sweet voice of his dearest friend, he jumped up and engulfed him in a tight, loving embrace. Krishna's voice was so laced with love that it filled Arjuna's heart with hope and energy. Arjuna held his hand tight and said, "What do you not know, Krishna? You know it all—my deepest thoughts and darkest desires. You know my intentions without me saying it. I am in this disguise because I could not think of any other way to go unnoticed here in Dwaraka. Besides, Balaram leads them; you know I cannot risk being spotted. Please help me unite with Subhadra, your sister ... please, if you want to." Krishna and Arjuna could pick up the thread of their relationship exactly where they had left it off years ago and start weaving new memories.

Love in a deep relationship is like a river that flows continuously despite people not visiting it for years.

Placing his arms around Arjuna's shoulder and pulling him closer, Krishna walked Arjuna to his chariot and rode off with him toward the most breathtaking side of the Raivataka mountains. The two friends spent the next few days soul-searching and bonding again. Assuring Arjuna that he would return with a plan, Krishna left him in the magnificent mountains and returned to Dwaraka.

Love at First Sight

The Vrishni clan's mountain-worshipping festival was around the corner. The people always went all out on this festival. They decorated the Raivataka mountain with bright gems and colorful flower garlands; their musicians and dancers performed passionately throughout the day as Vrishni heroes visited the Raivataka with their families and distributed gifts to thousands of brahmans. But something was different this time: Among the teeming Vrishnis watching the festivities was the incognito Arjuna. As he watched the illustrious Vrishni heroes ride past, his eyes fell on a divine beauty. His jaw dropped; his wide gaze lingered on a beautiful goddess passing by. He stood transfixed, his fragile heart skipping beat after beat. His heart told him that this goddess had to be Subhadra.

"Hey! Your attire and your expressions do not match!" The familiar voice from behind him startled Arjuna, snapping him out of the hypnotic trance. Krishna had returned and was having fun observing Arjuna's hopelessness. The fake mendicant understood exactly what Krishna meant. But he could not help himself. Mendicant or not, he had to know the name of the damsel who had punctured his heart and left him breathless. Krishna looked deep into Arjuna's smitten eyes. "She is the one—the same Subhadra your heart longs for." Arjuna immediately grabbed Krishna's hand, pleading, "O Krishna, do not tease me, please, I beg you. Instead, please guide me and tell me how to make her mine."

A loving relationship does not judge the wrong actions but focuses on the right intentions of a loved person.

Krishna smiled. "Subhadra is my half-sister. She is Sarana's sister. Knowing that you are besotted by her, would you want me to discuss this with my father Vasudeva?"

"O, Krishna, the abode of love that you are, please tell me the right way to approach this relationship. Please advise me on the best I can do to marry her. I trust you and leave it to you to show me the way forward. I'll do as you say."

Arjuna had felt such a deep connection with Subhadra that he did not want to let go of her. He really wanted her in his life. So, he pleaded with his friend to intervene, calm his pounding heart, and steer his turbulent emotions to the right shore.

A loving companionship can settle a disturbed mind like coconut coir can purify water in an unclean well.

Krishna pulled his hand away and took Arjuna away from the crowd to a more private and quieter place for a deep conversation on marriage. "Arjuna, you know, Vedic texts say that marriages are of eight kinds—some superior and some inferior.

- In a *brahma* marriage, the girl's father chooses a man for his daughter based on his character and family values and marries her off to him with great respect, blessings, and dowry.
- In a *daiva* marriage, the father bestows his daughter to the priest, who officiates a sacrifice on his behalf.
- *Prajapatya* is a private marriage with no ceremony or guests. The father offers his daughter to a man with all his blessings so that they may lead a *dharmic* life together.

These are all superior types of marriages.

Then there are these condemned, inferior types of marriages.

- An *arsha* marriage is more of a business transaction in which the father gives away his daughter to a man in exchange for some kind of valuable gift.
- In an asura marriage, the father just sells his daughter to a man.
- In a rakshasa marriage, a man abducts the woman from her house using violence and weapons against anyone coming in the way.
- A *pishaacha* marriage is really oppression and is the worst because the man compels a woman to live with him against her will.
- Finally, there is the *gandharva* marriage, which is entirely based on mutual love between two people and does not really need the family's consent. It is a marriage that celebrates love.

"I'd say the best kind of marriage is where two people fall in love with and remain committed to each other. Only when you are certain that Subhadra really desires you as much as you desire her should you even think of marrying her. The heart of a woman is very important in a marriage. I have an idea. If you follow my plan, you will surely find a way to win my sister's heart. I will make sure that you meet her and have enough time to connect with her. How you do it is all up to you."

Love is to a relationship what fragrance is to a flower; just as a flower loses its essence without fragrance, a relationship loses its essence without love.

A few moments later, Arjuna was sitting in a temple courtyard—meditating. As the Vrishnis passed by in small groups, they felt drawn towards the unfamiliar mystic. Balaram, Samba, Sarana, Pradyumna, and Gada all walked by, one after the other, impressed by the ascetic. Balaram was particularly captivated by him. *Something is so supernatural about this handsome sannyasi—the ash stripes across his body, his simple clothes, his majestic air, his eyes tightly shut to the outside world but seemingly wide open to his inner universe.* As Balaram assessed Arjuna, he was clueless that behind the poised and composed façade was a nervous wreck, afraid of his disguise being blown.

Krishna had warned Arjuna not to lose his nerve, especially if Balaram stopped to stare at him. Although his eyes were closed, Arjuna could feel Balaram's eyes on him.

Love requires showing courage on the outside, even when trembling on the inside.

Balaram noticed the mystic ascetic open his eyes slowly and look at him with compassion and confidence; he immediately folded his hands and bowed in front of the mystic. *This is a miracle! The great Balaram did not recognize me.*

Arjuna knew a beard and an attire change were superficial tools to conceal an identity that could fool most people, but probably not someone as observant as Balaram. He could have been caught easily, but Arjuna was pleasantly surprised. Lying prostrate in front of him in obeisance was the sharp-eyed and perceptive Balaram.

Balaram heartily welcomed Arjuna to Dwaraka, asking him animatedly about his travel plans and volunteering to make his stay in the city comfortable. Arjuna raised his hands with an air of authority and spoke in a voice very different from his own. He did not want his identity exposed. Not now, at least. "I have been traveling all over the world, and no stay has ever extended beyond three days. But then we have already entered *chaturmasa*, haven't we? So, I am considering living out the four months of the wet season here. Of all the places I have seen and been to, Raivataka has captured my soul. I feel calm and at ease. Even my meditation has become deeper since the day I arrived here. That says a lot about this place!"

How sincere, how genuine, how attractive, how intense his tapasya. He is so young yet so wise. I feel lucky to have the honor of hosting such an exalted soul. Balaram's silent admiration for the sage in front of him would have gone on longer had Krishna not made an out-of-the-blue appearance there. Balaram was not expecting Krishna. He quickly gathered his thoughts and introduced him to the traveling monk. "Oh, Enlightened One! Please meet my brother Krishna." Krishna warmly greeted him—as if meeting him for the first time. But the ascetic did not miss the naughty twinkle in Krishna's eyes. No words were exchanged, but codes were cracked.

Krishna had deliberately kept himself away from the scene of action. He wanted Balaram to be the one to meet the great ascetic first and develop a liking for him. He knew that his plans for Arjuna and Subhadra would be far smoother if this happened.

"You know, Krishna, this master has decided to honor our kingdom by spending four months here! Where do you think we should host him? Any suggestions?" With an indifferent smile, Krishna shrugged and said, "When my elder brother is here, who am I to suggest anything? It is inappropriate and offensive to do that as a younger sibling, isn't it?" Krishna's words made Balaram smile. *He is so humble.* Balaram could not have been prouder of Krishna's public gesture, which seemed to elevate his authority over Dwaraka a few notches higher.

The art of winning hearts is knowing when to speak and when to remain silent, when to be present and when to be obscure, when to suggest and when to encourage.

"Alright! The best place would be the garden house in Subhadra's palace. I will assign our sister, Subhadra, to ensure the care of the great saint.[2] She is an expert host and is very well-trained in the highest standards of hospitality."

This was exactly Krishna's plan. He was pleased with how perfect it was. But then he wanted to make it even more foolproof. So, he decided to add a dash of doubt. He pulled Balaram away from the crowd as if to reveal some secret and then whispered, "Do you really think it is safe to allow such a handsome young sage to stay in such proximity to our beautiful sister who, as you are aware, is of marriageable age? Look at his personality. So powerful. So eloquent. So charming. He has everything to steal a young woman's heart. I would say, do not make the mistake you are about to make. I strongly disapprove of this idea. But then again, you are the wise one and are always so insightful. I am sure you have thought everything through before arriving at this decision. It must be the most balanced and smart decision ever."

Many loving relationships can co-exist in harmony. Any relationship built on the tomb of another will soon be buried. Love is the ability to balance priorities sensitively.

---

[2] It was a common tradition at the time for young girls to be assigned to serve and look after the well-being of saintly or anointed people. This act of service was seen as an opportunity to earn the saints' blessings for a prosperous and happy future.

Krishna's little doubt train threw Balaram off. He became terribly upset that Krishna could even think this way about such an exalted sage. "Krishna! What audacity! How dare you talk this way about the great saint? Apologize right now! Ask the sage for forgiveness for your impudence and derogatory remarks. You need to be punished for this!"

Completely convinced that he was penalizing Krishna, Balaram assigned him the job of helping the ascetic settle in smoothly in the palace garden and ensuring all arrangements to make him immediately comfortable. Krishna smiled. The plan was working even better now! *Such a simpleton!* His brother's innocence floored Krishna. He remembered how he had always gotten his way with Balaram since the time they were children, just because he could always predict his brother's actions and reactions.

Understand people before trying to fathom relationships. This will help lay the deep foundation for building towering relationships.

With the disguised Arjuna now on his chariot, Krishna entered the city of Dwaraka. Arjuna was mesmerized by the splendor of Krishna's city. *Is this what heaven looks like?* Arjuna's eyes soaked in everything—the city's fervor, its never-ending festive mood, its happy citizens celebrating. *This must be heaven!*

Holding his friend's hand, Krishna first took Arjuna to his own palace. He introduced him to his two principal wives, Rukmini and Satyabhama. They smiled and welcomed their guest with effusive words of praise, almost speaking over each other. “We have heard so much about you.” “Yes, but we never had the chance of meeting you.” “Please consider this your home.” With all pleasantries done, the two friends made their way toward *the* moment.

Krishna led Arjuna to Subhadra’s palace. “Dear Sister, I assign under your care this great exalted traveling sage. O Master! Meet my sister, Subhadra, your host throughout your stay in our city.”

Subhadra was clueless about the person behind the disguise. In fact, she did not even realize it was a disguise. She was all ears as Krishna continued instructing her on what arrangements she needed to make. “Brother Balaram is very keen that this sage be well taken care of. I trust you will keep his trust in you to host him well.” As he said this, Krishna turned toward Arjuna with a sly smile and then left the two to settle into their roles as the guest and the host.

Partner in Love

From the moment he saw Subhadra, Arjuna was drowning in boundless bliss. Watching her each day as she went about her daily chores was like washing his eyes with nectar. *Such grace! Such beauty!* Subhadra took her host responsibilities quite seriously. She was sincere and took care of all his requirements. She was also so intuitive, arranging things for Arjuna even before he asked for something. Everything she did was meticulous and artistic. Arjuna felt most comfortable and cared for because of the impeccable hospitality.

Arjuna’s love for Subhadra grew exponentially each time he

met her—the compounding effect of each meeting becoming more difficult for him to handle. He would sigh loudly as soon as she left his presence. Subhadra could not get a read on the sadness she saw on Arjuna's face every time she left. Arjuna, however, would steal a glance at her whenever he saw her playing in the garden with her friends. The more he saw her, the more he wanted to see her. He was addicted to her now.

The sign of love is in paying attention to details.

Arjuna was a household name in Dwaraka—an urban legend. Every person knew of and spoke about his heroic acts. Mothers used Arjuna's obedience and discipline as examples for their children to follow. Warriors discussed his battlefield accomplishments with each other and took inspiration from him. Archery schools placed him on a pedestal and referred to him as the epitome of practice and perfection in the art and science of warfare. Elders blessed youngsters to grow up to achieve success and fame like Arjuna. The young women often teased each other about Arjuna as he was the one every woman secretly desired.

Words and vibrations about Arjuna surrounded Subhadra, and she was fascinated: *Who is this person who has rocked Dwaraka, the place that is home to the most magnificent Krishna?* Even her cousin Gada often spoke about him. And when Krishna told her something about him, he seemed to have five mouths! His vocabulary became inexhaustible when talking about this special friend. Subhadra felt irresistibly and inexplicably drawn to Arjuna without ever having seen or met him. She could feel a special bond in her heart.

Yet, since the day this ascetic unexpectedly walked into her life, she began experiencing strange emotions. She always felt his eyes on her from somewhere, even when she could not see him anywhere. When she was in his presence, his stare was so intense that she could not look him in the eye. Some strange thoughts began crossing her mind. "*He does not seem very sannyasi-like. He looks as strong as a warrior. Are those bowstring and arrow marks on his arms and shoulders?*" Every time Subhadra saw him, she tried to find answers to these questions plaguing her mind. From the numerous stories she had heard of Arjuna, she gathered that he was ambidextrous and could use the bow with both his hands. More doubts began creeping into her mind. *What do those bow-and-arrow marks on both the arms of the ascetic mean? Was he ambidextrous like Arjuna? Or was he Arjuna?* This thought unsettled her, but she decided to brush it aside. She knew she would have to investigate it soon.

Knowledge about someone is like filling a container. The more the knowledge, the larger the container. The larger the container, the deeper the love. The deeper the love, the stronger the bond.

The three-and-half months passed by quickly. One day, Subhadra suddenly found the moment she had been waiting for—time alone with the ascetic. They began discussing travel.

Over these past months, the two had become comfortable enough to have long discourses on various topics. Subhadra enjoyed every lengthy exchange with him and was impressed each time. She thought his wisdom was refreshing. His perspectives on life totally resonated with hers.

"Since you have traveled the world, could you tell me something about the most fascinating places you have visited ... the most interesting people you have met?"

Subhadra's question set Arjuna off on a long monologue about his adventures, almost as if he was dying to share these with her.

"Have you ever visited Indraprastha?"

His eyes lit up at the mention of Indraprastha. "Of course, of course!"

"Have you met the great Pandavas and my aunt Kunti?"

"Of course! Not only have I met them, but I also know them well!"

"Would you, by chance, know anything about where Arjuna could be? I have heard he has been away from Indraprastha for a long time. From what I have heard, it seems like he has been on some kind of pilgrimage for the past twelve years. Have your paths ever crossed with the great hero during your travels?"

Initiating a discussion is like gently opening a box full of surprises. One should be prepared for what spills out of it.

Arjuna broke into a smile. "O yes! Not only have I met him, but I also happen to know exactly where he is right now!"

"Where? Where? Where is he?" Subhadra leapt up. She was not the most subtle person when it came to expressing curiosity.

The ascetic inched closer to her and said in his low-pitched, raspy voice, "Right now, Arjuna is staring at the most gorgeous woman in the world. He is dressed up as an ascetic and living a very difficult life, all because he wants to woo her. He is right in front of the woman he desires madly, but she is clueless about his disguise and cannot recognize him. He is dying to express his love for her right this moment. He is not certain if the one he loves will accept him, but he is very certain he cannot breathe or live without her."

Vulnerability facilitates the birth of love.

Subhadra was blushing red. *What?! Is this ascetic here whom I have been serving, the hero Arjuna—the one I am secretly head-over-heels in love with?* Subhadra was struggling to gain composure. Her emotions seemed to be spiraling out of control. *Did he just propose to me so shamelessly?* Subhadra stood up without a word and walked away. She even found it hard to blink. Her body was burning, but she was shivering. *What is this? Excitement? Fear? Joy? Exhilaration?* Subhadra had no idea. She rushed to her bedroom and plopped on the bed, staying there alone and listless for hours. She only had the sound of her breathing and the agonizing pain in her pounding heart for company. Subhadra was lovesick!

Her family was in a state of panic. The royal physician could not diagnose her illness. All her vitals seemed normal, but she did not. When the physicians gave up, Krishna came to the rescue. He appeared to know exactly what was ailing his sister.

Subhadra did not know of Krishna's involvement in the matter, so she stayed in her room sulking and worrying. *I cannot even tell my family what my heart desires—not when the man I love is dressed as a sannyasi. My heart hurts that I could not even tell Arjuna!*

Fear and love often appear together for only the deepest darkness can help appreciate the brightest light.

The all-knowing Krishna spoke to the family. "All of you should visit the temple of Lord Shiva on the island nearby and perform a fifteen-day worship for her good health." He told his parents, Devaki and Vasudev, to lead this worship. Balaram immediately agreed, too. Soon, everyone was set to embark on this little "heal Subhadra" pilgrimage to the island. Krishna, too, had to accompany them. He was family, after all.

But just before stepping out, Krishna quickly met Subhadra and sprang a plan on her. "You now have all the time to recover and connect with Arjuna closely. You have twelve days to decide and tell him what your heart wants. If you choose him, then there is an auspicious wedding date at the end of those twelve days. See you then."

Give love space to grow. Give people space to understand the worth of your love. Being too close can stifle thoughts.

Love Forever

Arjuna waited patiently till the twelfth day before approaching Subhadra. He was a tangled ball of emotions. By this time, Subhadra had gained composure. She knew that Krishna was on her side. Arjuna spoke yet again. This time, not as the man hiding his identity but as a man confronting the woman of his dreams. "I love you madly. I cannot imagine a life without you in it. I will take good care of you, shower you with endless affection, and be by your side till the end of time and beyond. My heart deeply wants to be with you. Because Krishna said we should unite today, I am here again, begging you to be mine. Only if you wish, though. I am sure you know that it is perfectly alright for us kshatriyas to elope and marry. In fact, it is rather chivalrous if consensual. Would you be mine and light up my life?"

Genuineness energizes a relationship.

Overwhelmed with joy, Subhadra burst into tears. She could

not believe that the world's greatest hero—the Arjuna—was confessing his love to her. *I must be really fortunate!* She nodded in agreement and quickly hung her head to hide her shyness. Half-crying, half-smiling, she could not really contain this new and heavenly feeling of joy that she was carrying in her heart. The lovers exchanged silent glances—the smiles fixed on their faces.

Silent gestures can be louder than empty words.

Once certain that Subhadra was all his—heart and soul—Arjuna wasted no time giving her instructions on the way forward. "Do not be afraid. Ready a chariot yoked with the swiftest of horses." Subhadra sprang into action right away. When she reached the palace, she noticed Krishna—her dear, thoughtful brother—had left behind his own chariot yoked with his favorite horses, Saibya, Sugriva, Valaahaka, and Meghapushpa. Subhadra hopped on the chariot and deftly maneuvered it toward Arjuna's hamlet.

Gone was the ascetic in mendicant attire, fake beard, and mustache. Instead, emerging from the little hut was this well-built, clean-faced, handsome prince in all his glory. Dressed in royal clothes, hair set with scented oils, and flashing a chest armor, Arjuna looked every bit the rugged and powerful hero Subhadra had imagined him to be—only a million times more handsome. His beaming smile melted her heart. She had spent so many nights dreaming about this hero. Arjuna jumped into the chariot and sat next to her. Choosing not to take over the reins, he left Subhadra to continue riding the chariot.

Subhadra signaled the horses to run faster. Krishna had stacked the most powerful weapons on that chariot. Arjuna armed himself with a formidable bow and a quiver of arrows, ready for any onslaught. Whizzing through the streets of Dwaraka, the couple disappeared from the city as the chariot exited the city gates in the blink of an eye.

"Love" and "control" cannot coexist; "love" and "respect" are inseparable.

Balaram, all livid, rushed to Krishna. "You knew it, did you not? The abductor is your friend Arjuna, the not-so-exalted-one in disguise! You had to know!" Krishna smiled. "Had I not told you initially to think twice before arranging the ascetic's stay at Subhadra's palace? I had even warned you. But then you were overconfident about your judgment."

"I refuse to believe this. I know you were in on this. How many more such tricks have you planned? I will destroy Arjuna, and all the Pandavas and their city, Indraprastha, if that is what it comes down to." Krishna slowly approached him and placed his reassuring hand on his shoulder. "My dear brother, do not be angry," he said in a soft, pacifying tone that starkly contrasted the mischievous voice earlier. "If you decide to destroy the Pandavas, no one can save them. But before you put your plans into action, spare some thought for the charioteer's identity. Have you asked your guards that? Your people have fed you only half the information. Then let me tell you that it was Subhadra. If she were the charioteer, how could Arjuna really abduct her?

Does it not imply she eloped with him? She has chosen him, my dear brother. Now think again, which warrior in this world other than the mighty Arjuna could make a better groom for our beautiful sister? It would be in the best interest of both families to allow them to marry. There could be no better allies than the Pandavas."

Krishna's composure calmed Balaram down, and the logic appealed to him. Balaram decided against pursuing Arjuna and allowed him to reach Indraprastha with Subhadra. Once the young couple settled down, they would go to Indraprastha with a wedding team and conduct the couple's wedding with splendor.

It takes a calm mind to differentiate between true and fake love. Anger torches out all rationality but fuels judgment and scepticism.

As Balaram's anger was losing steam in Dwaraka, Subhadra and Arjuna entered Indraprastha. He had already informed his elder brother, Yudhishthir, about his plan and sought his blessings before eloping with Subhadra. Arjuna told Subhadra, "You must enter the city on your own and meet Draupadi. Do not tell her about us." Krishna had already trained her on how to approach this sensitive matter. Subhadra dressed as a simple cowherdess and entered Draupadi's palace. As the innocent-looking girl entered the palace, she immediately caught Draupadi's attention. A few questions later, Draupadi seemed very interested. "Oh, so you are Krishna's sister! This makes me so happy!" Subhadra fell at Draupadi's feet. Draupadi was quite impressed by the girl's simplicity and respect. She pulled her up and hugged her before taking her to her room—the two talked for hours about Krishna. Draupadi blessed Subhadra, "May you find a great hero to be your husband. May you have a son who proves to be the supreme hero."

Outside, people were welcoming Arjuna. Everyone rushed to the returning Pandava hero. Falling at Yudhishthir's feet, Arjuna briefed him about his exile period, his affair at Dwaraka, and his desire to marry Subhadra. As he mentioned Subhadra, he turned toward Draupadi, expecting to see an angry face. Instead, she was smiling. "I have already met the beautiful Subhadra. No one can resist her charms, not even I."

Almost all of Dwaraka was at the festive and splendorous wedding. Subhadra and Arjuna could not be more grateful for Krishna's guidance through their journey of love. Without him by their side, their love would never have won. Krishna helped them cross barriers and build bridges. He helped love triumph. They fell at Krishna's feet for his blessings.

Only a good conductor with expertise in
bringing loving people together can make the
symphony of life sound melodious.

3

THE SOLUTIONIST

5.77.11

लोकस्य नान्यतो वृत्तिः पाण्डवान्यत्र कर्मणः ।
एवंबुद्धिः प्रवर्तेत फलं स्यादुभयान्वये ॥

Lokasya naanyato vrittih paandavaanyatra karmanah
Evambuddhih pravarteta phalam syaadubhayaanvaye

"O son of Pandu! One must remember that action is unavoidable. Fate aligns with effort to bring the results of one's deeds."

Every lock has a key. Every problem has a solution. A solutionist holds the key to unlocking life's deadbolts.

A Visit Like No Other

The cosmic traveler Narada *muni*'s visit was a moment to remember. Yudhishthir's joy knew no bounds. This special visit was the crescendo of the celebration of the inauguration of Maya sabha—a hall of illusions—Indraprastha's new assembly hall. Maya, the king of the *danavas*,[3] created it for the Pandavas, in return for Arjuna having saved his life.

Everyone was welcome, but this celestial visit added to the grandeur of the occasion. Visitors from across the universe had descended on the city to celebrate this unique piece of architecture. Narada's arrival was symbolic of the supreme validation Yudhishthir sought. His assembly hall had sent ripples across the halls of the powers that be of the universe.

Filled with anticipation, Yudhishthir requested Narada to describe the assembly halls of the greatest entities in this universe. The intent was to see how his hall measured against the best in the universe. Captivated, the audience listened to Narada's vivid descriptions of the interiors, elaborating on the specialty of each celestial place he had seen. They could not help but draw comparisons with the Maya sabha. As Narada described these breathtaking halls of Indra, Brahma, Varuna, Yama, and others, he also shared little anecdotes about the exalted beings he met there.

"... and the Indra sabha is grand, lustrous, opulent, and magnificent. He built it himself. Many eminent rishis, gods, deities, and other celestial beings wait upon Indra. The assembly

---

[3] demons

also has all the forces of nature—clouds, rains, wind, fire, … and … sharing the throne … King Harishchandra. Visvakarma, the architect of the resplendent, joyous, blissful, and harmonious Yama sabha, created a paradise-like assembly free of pain and suffering. This realm of the dead is home to many legendary kings—Yayati, Nahusha, Shantanu, and Pandu. Varuna's sabha, Pushkaramalini is also splendid and grand … pure … this realm of the waters and oceans is home to many celestial beings, earthly kings, …"

As everyone listened to Narada's vivid descriptions, they imagined the beauty and grandeur of these beautiful halls and compared them to the Maya sabha. Yudhishthir, however, was not so as focused on the halls as on the noble characters the sage had met. A particular anecdote about a king unsettled him.

"O Sage, while most great kings of the earth had reached Yama sabha, why is King Harishchandra in heaven? Not only is he in heaven, but he also shares the seat with King Indra!" Yudhishthir was too shocked by this little detail in Narada's narration about the great sabhas. *This changes everything I have ever known about the concept of pious living*!

Narada smiled. *Huh! How did he catch that bit? I had underplayed this in my description, yet his keen ears...*

"O great sage! What deeds did King Harishchandra perform for him to find a place of honor next to Indra? Even more surprising, what opportunity did his pious father, Pandu, and other exalted kings miss that they are now in the realm of the dead instead?"

Often the biggest ideas lie hidden in the smallest of details. The best teachers hide deep insights in their teachings for their best students to sift through the plethora of information to unearth wisdom.

"Rajasuya *yagna*! Your father has requested that I tell you to perform the *yagna* and help extract him from the realm of the dead. With Krishna by your side, nothing is impossible."

Narada had stealthily planted a seed in Yudhishthir's mind. It kept growing until it became a tree full of foliage, arching to encompass the whole world.

I know the Rajasuya yagna will be the first step toward expanding my kingdom across the length and breadth of the world. But I do not feel ready yet. A still-unsure Yudhishthir called his most important advisors and friends together for a brainstorming session. Everyone seemed optimistic, but he wanted a realistic opinion. He turned to Krishna, "You tell me the truth."

Good advice is annoying because the truth is annoying.

Pondering for a moment, Krishna said, "If something makes me think twice about the Rajasuya *yagna*, it would be one name—Jarasandha. Jarasandha is not just a name. He is a strategic force. He has formidable allies—Sishupala of Chedi, Rukmi of Vidarbha, Paundraka of Paundra, and Bhagadatta of Pragjyotisha. He is one brute force and the sworn enemy of the Vrishni dynasty. I have fought more than seventeen wars with him. Each time, he has returned with a bigger army. His torment forced us to move from Mathura to Dwaraka overnight. When you announce the Rajasuya *yagna*, Duryodhana will first join hands with Jarasandha. Imagine the Kauravas, backed by Bhishma, Dronacharya, Kripa, and Karna, standing shoulder-to-shoulder with Jarasandha and all his friends—all their weapons pointed toward you. You must also know that Jarasandha has captured ninety-eight kings from various kingdoms. He plans to offer all their heads in a mass human sacrifice. If you can somehow obliterate him, no one will dare oppose you. The Rajasuya will be smooth and uninterrupted. But if you leave him be, this *yagna* will remain a pipe dream."

Strategic thinking is a magical balance between analysis and practicality.

Such crystal-clear advice! Yudhishthir was amazed. After Krishna's explanation, his doubt was reinforced. "I'd rather abandon the idea itself!" Bhima, unlike him, was very confident. "What we cannot achieve with force, we can achieve with wisdom." Bhima's overenthusiasm seemed amusing to Krishna. He explained, "You are right. But this will not be as easy as you imagine. Shiva has bestowed a special favor upon Jarasandha, who already has many powerful allies. Being attacked by such forceful entities is no different from trying to make it ashore by swimming across a river filled with alligators. But then, if you perform this *yagna*, you can save the lives of the innocent kings. The risk might be worth it."

The most successful people in this world are those who risk stepping into darkness with only the light of hope.

Yudhishthir was hesitant. *I do not want to lose my two eyes, Arjuna and Bhima. I do not want to lose my heart, Krishna, either.* The adventure-loving Arjuna said, "A kshatriya is born to fight against wrong. If ours is the path of righteousness, all aid will come to us. The gods will not favor a king on the wrong path. Such a king is already walking toward his doom. As keepers of dharma, it is our duty to rid this world of evil monsters."

Krishna added, "Death can come at any time. Staying away from wars does not guarantee immortality. Humans have too short a life span to decide on the impact of their existence. Life or death hardly matters when fighting for a good cause. If you win, this world will celebrate you. If you die, the heavens will celebrate you."

Reckless living and riskless living are two extremes of meaningless living.

A Birth Like No Other

"Who is this monster? He is still alive despite several wars against you. He is surely not someone ordinary. Just as moths never can survive the flames, no warrior can withstand your wrath. Educate us about this obstacle so that we can chalk out a strategy to destroy him and achieve our goal." Yudhishthir was keen to know and quizzed Krishna.

"Brihadratha—a powerful, influential king—controlled Magadha from the capital city at the foothills of Girivraja. He had many powerful kshatriya traits and a very dharmic mindset. Just as the rays of the morning sun light up the earth, his fame reached every nook and cranny of the kingdom. Just as moonlight permeates darkness with its bright rays, his kingdom fills everyone's hearts with hope.

Brihadratha was married to the twin princesses from the kingdom of Kashi. While hope and happiness shone through his entire kingdom, the pain of childlessness eclipsed his own life."

The cycle of hope is like the cycle of rain—water rises from the oceans to become clouds to rain on land. Hope rises from the giver so that the receiver can shower it on others.

Krishna continued with the story, "Disillusioned that his lineage would end with him, Brihadratha retreated into the forest with his wives. He met a mystic sage Chandakaushika. The sage was shocked to see a young king retiring to the forest. One day, as they all sat under a mango tree telling him their woes, the sage realized the root of the king's pain and decided to intervene.

"Suddenly, a mango fell on the king's lap. The sage picked up that mango and said, 'This special mango will bless you with a child. The wife who eats this will soon bear a child.' Brihadratha was so excited with this life-transforming encounter that he rushed back to his kingdom with his wives and the precious fruit. In all fairness, he cut the mango in half and gave each half to each wife. Unwittingly, the king had modified the sage's instructions.

"Not long after, the queens delivered. But the queens each gave birth to only one half of a child, just as the halved mango they had eaten. The halves were exactly symmetrical but no more than lumps of flesh. The nurse was convinced that the queens had given birth to monsters. On the king's instructions, the nurse wrapped the pieces of flesh in separate cloth bundles and flung them outside the city gates.

Making decisions on half-baked knowledge is foolish.

"That night, a terrible *rakshasi*, Jara, prowling around the area looking for flesh to satisfy her hunger pangs, gravitated toward the two pieces of discarded flesh. She was thrilled to see the tenderest of human flesh wrapped in the cloth bundles. She flung the two pieces of flesh over her shoulder, inadvertently placing them next to each other. As she continued walking to her dwelling, she heard a baby cry. She carefully set down the bundle and opened it to discover the most delicate baby staring at her with big, teary eyes. Instantly, her motherly instincts kicked in. She could not think of harming that tiny tot now.

She did some digging around and discovered that the baby was Brihadratha's offspring. She walked up to the royal court to tell him about her experience. 'The two pieces miraculously joined, and this is what I have now!" she said as she handed the baby over to the king. 'I am so grateful to you, Jara, for sacrificing cannibalistic instinct and returning my baby to me safely. So, as a gesture of gratitude, I name this baby Jarasandha after you.'

Every human harbors a demonic instinct,
and every demon harbors a human instinct.
Demonize a human and humanize a demon
only after carefully observing, considering, and
deciphering the motivation.

Just when he had named the baby, sage Chandakaushika entered the palace hall. 'This child will be extraordinary and cannot be easily defeated by anyone. He will receive the favor of Lord Shiva and become indomitable.'"

After Krishna's narration of Jarasandha's story, the same thought ran across the Pandavas' minds: *How can someone who has defeated death itself and is blessed by Lord Shiva be destroyed?*

"A one-on-one combat!" Krishna said, sensing their shock.

When the problem is intricate, it is best to break it down.

Placing his hand on the shoulders of a stunned Yudhishthir, Krishna said, "Send Bhima and Arjuna along with me. I promise to protect them and return victorious." The three left for Magadha as soon as Yudhishthir relented. They crossed the rivers Sarayu and Gandaki before finally reaching Mithila. They then crossed the Ganga and made their way until they could spot the Girivraja mountain in the distance.

Outside the capital city stood an ornate Shiva temple. The three travelers entered the temple as warriors but stepped out of it as brahmans. The saffron robes, sandalwood paste on their bodies, the garlands around their necks all seemed to make them stand out instead of making them inconspicuous. Although dressed as brahmans, their gait was warrior-like. They seemed like lions, casually prowling the city roads leading toward the palace. They spotted many omens that spelled doom for the king.

When they almost reached the palace gate, they took a sudden detour. Within moments, the guards inside heard a thud. Sensing a security threat, they rushed with their weapons raised to the wall by the palace garden. Standing there smiling were three brahmans. *Had they just jumped over the wall into the palace garden? Why did they not walk in through the gate instead?* The baffled guards greeted the brahmans, ushering them toward the palace. Their king treated all brahmans with utmost respect.

Problems are games people take too seriously.
Games are problems people solve as they play.
Just as it is futile to intensify games, it is
unnecessary to amplify problems. It is best to
perceive problems as playing a challenging game.

They took the trio into an exquisite room and served them food and refreshments while they waited for the king. Then someone came in and announced: "The king is busy with some rituals. His Majesty will visit you exactly at midnight."

As promised, Jarasandha made a grand entry exactly at midnight and sat down with his guests. Even before they could introduce themselves, Jarasandha made some observations. "You are dressed as brahmans, but those flowers and perfumes you have on you prove that you are not what you appear to be. Besides, your method of entry into my palace suggests that you are not friends. Only enemies consciously choose not to enter through the main gate. Then again, you have neither had a morsel nor a sip of anything. The scars on your broad shoulders scream that you are kshatriyas disguised as brahmans. Now tell me, who are you? What do you want from me?"

Krishna spoke in a charming yet light-hearted manner. "Yes, Jarasandha. You are right. We are indeed your enemies. From the moment we entered your kingdom, we have deliberately made it obvious with every move and every step. We are here to fight you."

People convey through actions what they do not want to express through words.

The brazen confession. Jarasandha was taken aback. "When I do not even know you, how can you be my enemy?"

"You are the enemy of humanity. You have imprisoned so many innocent kings for a human sacrifice. That alone is a loud declaration of enmity against every upholder of dharma. You know us very well, Jarasandha. This is Arjuna, the third Pandava; this is Bhima, the second brother; and I am Krishna, your old enemy. We are here to challenge you to a one-on-one duel with any one of us."

"Hahaha! Look at this! You, who fled away from fear of me seventeen times, will challenge me here now? The same one who has been hiding on an island in the middle of the ocean in fear of me has come here to fight me? That is some courage you have to even attempt this! Did it take you so long to muster this courage? Do these young lackeys you have dragged along boost your ego enough to come here to face me? Make no mistake. I am not like your uncle Kamsa whom you killed so treacherously. I am Jarasandha, the undefeatable one, favored by the gods. You are nothing but a loud, rumbling autumn cloud that brings no rain. If the three of you are here for a fight, I will give you one. But I will not fight you, Krishna. I have proven you a coward far too many times. It is beneath me to duel with you. I will not fight Arjuna. He is a kid. Bhima seems worthy. I will fight him."[4]

Jarasandha was confident of victory, but that confidence did not totally blind him. He, too, had seen many omens warning of doom. So, as a precaution and not to leave his kingdom unattended, he crowned his son Sahadeva as king in his absence. He then began preparing for the combat.

All of Magadha was there to witness this mammoth clash. The arena was brimming with thousands expecting a nail-biting finish. Bhima's gigantic size had already created quite a stir in the city. While every wrestler vouched that no one was as muscular as him, they were equivocal in their confidence in Jarasandha's strength and power.

A Battle Like No Other

As Bhima walked into the wrestling arena, the crowd cheered him. He was their king's enemy, but they could not resist being drawn to his personality. Jarasandha walked in to a standing ovation—out of both admiration and fear—from his people. Their king was their hero. The collision from the first clash between two giants sounded like a loud thunderclap. The drummers increased the tempo with every move and movement of the rough and vigorous combat, adding to the drama at the

---

[4] This story has a Dwaraka version and a Maghadha version—a Krishna version, and a Jarasandha version. Every story has two versions—that of the victor and that of the vanquished. With each version, the vanquished and the victor are interchanged. No version is right or wrong. Both only reveal the mindset of the storyteller.

center of the arena. Soon, the two were pounding mercilessly at each other, blood oozing out of their multiple wounds. Both were determined to break each other's bones and resolves. They were neither tired nor disappointed. The combat kept becoming wilder with each blow.

Every fight between two entities is first a clash of ideologies, second a clash of egos, and third, a clash of fists.

The first day ended in a draw. For fourteen more days and nights, the two men kept baying for each other's blood. Through this violent fortnight, Krishna was with Bhima every step of the way, encouraging him and reminding him of his ancestry and valor. Slowly Bhima began gaining an upper hand over Jarasandha. By the end of day fourteen, Bhima managed to totally overpower Jarasandha and pin him to the ground.

Jarasandha lay on the ground face up, Bhima's leg pinning his chest down. Bhima then grabbed one of Jarasandha's legs with his mighty arms and began to pull it apart. Everyone stood silent as they heard the loud crack of a breaking spine and the loudest cry ever. Bhima was roaring while ripping Jarasandha apart like a cloth into two halves. A collective gasp escaped the audience. They had never seen anything this gruesome. Bhima began pounding his chest to announce his victory. He began circling the arena, his hands raised, basking in self-glory. The audience's expressions invigorated him—the shock, the dismay, the disbelief, the adoration, the admiration ... Suddenly, Bhima noticed the expressions had switched to shock again. *Why?*

Within seconds, everyone had their palms over their faces or mouths. Screaming in disbelief and staring in horror at each other, they began pointing toward Bhima. Bhima could not process this sudden change. His eyes then rested on Arjuna, who was frantically gesturing him to turn around. It was only then that he realized the crowd was not looking at him but something behind him. He quickly turned around; his jaws dropped to the ground. The one he had just shredded into two was now standing in front of him in one piece. As if nothing had ever happened at all. He had a wicked grin on his face. *Impossible*! *How could a dead man come back to life just like that?*

In a fit of frustrated aggression, Bhima barged into his resurrected opponent. After exchanging a few violent knocks, Bhima pinned him down again. Even as he was ripping apart yet again, the evil grin on Jarasandha's face was unmissable. It was as if he was not afraid to die, as if he was in partnership with Death. Regardless, Bhima tore him in half, again. No sooner than he had tossed the halves aside, the pieces, through some strong magnetic pull, began drawing closer until firmly attached together. Once attached, the pieces fused and became one, without any trace of dissection. Jarasandha was upright again, back to his formidable self. *He seems immortal!* By now, Bhima had become helpless. He turned toward Krishna as a bewildered child looking toward its mother for comfort and confidence.

A moment of prayer is all it takes to prevent helplessness from sliding into hopelessness.

Krishna simply bent over and picked up a leaf, held it in front of his face, split it in half, and flung the pieces in opposite directions—the left piece to the right and the right piece to his left. Then, he crossed his arms around his chest and smiled at Bhima. *Ah, right!*[5]

A Death Like No Other

All signs of bewilderment had disappeared from Bhima's face when he turned around to look Jarasandha in the eye. *Something has changed!* Even before Jarasandha could entirely register what shifted, Bhima had launched the final kill. Jarasandha lay on the ground, face up, but this time truly at the mercy of Bhima, with all hopes of a comeback gone forever. He sensed his game was up. He knew Krishna had played this well.

Bhima was merciless this time, ripping him apart with more vigor. He held the symmetrically bifurcated body parts in both his hands for all to see. The gore was too much for the audience. The collective whimpers and gasps reached a crescendo when Bhima crossed his hands and flung the two parts in opposite directions. He stood there almost as if hugging himself and declaring his majestic win.

---

[5] In his most helpless state, Bhima offered a silent prayer to Krishna. Krishna reciprocated with a small sign, which became the solution to all his problems. This is exactly what we need to follow in life—when at your most vulnerable state, offer a little prayer, and wait for a sign of hope from God.

Insight is the buried treasure between a problem and a solution. The moment you find it, you can unravel the most complicated of problems. Until you find that insight, solutions to even the simplest problems seem elusive.

All eyes were glued to the two pieces lying on the ground. That emptiness in the bloody eyeballs and the eerie stillness in the heavy atmosphere silently screamed out the verdict of the duel. A tense pause. Then the moment of realization. The crowds erupted as they rose to their feet, joyous and anxious. The mighty Jarasandha had finally fallen. Suddenly everyone was worried about security. *What next? What happens to us?* With the king dead, the kingdom now belonged to the enemy. Bhima seemed too ruthless a ruler.

Krishna walked to the center of the arena and calmed everyone down. "You have nothing to worry. You are all safe. Your new king will continue to be Jarasandha's son, Sahadeva. But going forward, Magadha will follow the dharmic tenets, a huge step away from autocratic *adharmic* rule."

Once he calmed the crowd, Krishna hopped onto Jarasandha's chariot with Bhima and Arjuna, and immediately made their way to the Girivraja peak where the king had kept all the kings captive. The trio unlocked all the prison doors one by one, setting many innocent kings free. The kings profusely thanked their rescuers. They could not believe that their rescuers wanted nothing in return for them and felt truly grateful. Krishna had invited all of them to attend King Yudhishthir's Rajasuya *yagna* in Indraprastha. Promising to be there, all the kings returned to their kingdoms. Everyone felt as if they had returned from hell. On their way back, they promised themselves that they would make the best use of this second chance and live a dharmic life in service to society and God.

After coronating Sahadeva, Krishna took time aside to counsel the boy. "Your father Jarasandha was a glorious warrior and king, but then he lost everything he had earned by misusing his power. Use your greatness for acts of service to society. Use your gentleness and your father's legacy for a dharmic purpose." The job done, Krishna and his cousins returned to Indraprastha.

Chaos outside is a reflection of the chaos inside.

Indraprastha regaled in Bhima's victory over Jarasandha. The trio became heroes all over again. Yudhishthir could not thank Krishna enough for eliminating the biggest obstacle to the Rajasuya *yagna*. Dharma had won.

Heart over Head

Krishna addresses the fear within the person rather than the chaos outside. His conversations are deep, therapeutic, foundational, directional, and principle centric. Careful attention to his words draws one toward him and makes one feel deeply connected with him in ways beyond words can describe. He believes in winning hearts, not winning kingdoms.

4

THE ALL-WITNESSING LORD

5.91.24

नाहं कामान्न संरम्भान्न द्वेषान्नार्थकारणात् ।
नाहेतुवादाल्लोभाद्वा धर्मं जह्यां कथञ्चन ॥

Naaham kaamaanna samrambhaanna
dveshaannaarthakaaranaat
Nahetuvaadaallobhaadva dharmam jahyaam
kathanchana

"I will not be controlled by desire, anger, hatred, or wealth. I will never forsake righteousness for selfish gain or greed."

Do everything you have to do, but not with greed, not with ego, not with lust, not with envy; but with love, compassion, humility, and devotion.

The Hall of Fame

The Khandava forest fire had razed everything to the ground. No one imagined anything could ever be built on the ashes of a once-thriving forest. Yet, what rose from the ashes was an extravagant and opulent assembly hall that became the foundation for a new kingdom—Indraprastha—and new rulers—the Pandavas.

The name Ajatashatru—the one who has no enemy, just found its way to Yudhishthir. He did not wear the mantle of the king of Indraprastha lightly. His was the rule of benevolence, kindness, and comfort. He cared for everyone as if they were family—so much that other kings felt comforted enough by his existence not to hate him. Bhima's rule was fair and unbiased. Arjuna was Savyasachi, the ambidextrous one. He leveraged his ability to use both hands equally skillfully to protect those who surrendered to Yudhishthir's sovereignty. Sahadeva was the master administrator who managed everything flawlessly. The youngest, Nakula's humility and effortless modesty won over all who met him.

Leaders who force, win only hands; leaders who inspire, win heads; leaders who impact, win hearts.

Indraprastha flourished under the Pandavas with dharma as its bedrock. All trades thrived, and natural disasters or anything of harm did not touch the kingdom. The treasury became full enough for a hundred years or more. Safe in the knowledge that the coffers were overflowing, Yudhishthir felt ready for the challenging Rajasuya *yagna*. Everyone in the assembly hall felt the same. Just then, Krishna stepped into the courtroom, affirming their confidence. He brought immense wealth as an offering for Yudhishthir's hyper *yagna*, allaying every doubt the Pandavas might have had. "Thank you, Krishna, for your encouragement and showing us the way forward." The Pandavas felt extremely grateful. Hands folded, Yudhishthir asked, "O Master of the Universe, may I begin the *yagna*?"

Prosperity comes with an abundance mindset and a genuine desire to help those around you. Wishing abundance for others brings abundance beyond expectation to self.

"I am here to participate in the *yagna*. I promise to follow your every command, Yudhishthir, and help you with the completion of this great ceremony." The moment the Pandavas got Krishna's go-ahead, Sahadeva plunged into the arrangement process, starting from gathering material and ingredients for the *yagna*. The great sages Vyas, Yajnavalkya, and Dhaumya became officiating priests. Swift messengers delivered the invitation to everyone across the universe. Everyone in Indraprastha, rank and status notwithstanding, received a special invite.

Yudhishthir took his seat at the sacred altar in the presence of thousands of spectators and brahmans. "Nakula, visit

Hastinapur, request the presence of Bhishma, Dronacharya, Dhritarashtra, and Kripacharya, and all our cousins.

These esteemed guests from Hastinapur and kings from every corner of the universe began arriving to witness Indraprastha's splendid festival. *From burned down land to this?! Beautiful! Such an astounding transformation! The epicenter of global affairs.*

Everyone participating was given accommodation—their houses stacked with food, luxurious comforts, and carefully selected furniture. Everyone had whatever they needed or wanted without even asking.

Good leaders are aware of and address the feelings, interests, and problems of those around them.

Tasks and Talents

It was customary to involve close relatives and friends in the planning and execution of the sacrifice and assign them to specific groups with the requisite skills and attributes. Because Bhima loved food, he was made head chef. Dushasana was in charge of serving the food. Ashwatthama was entrusted with managing the brahmans, and Sanjaya was asked to greet and honor the visiting kings. Bhishma and Dronacharya, the team's most senior and knowledgeable members, were made reviewers so they could use their extensive knowledge and astute observation skills to assess the arrangements so that nothing was overlooked. Kripacharya was appointed to guard the jewels and gems and to distribute benefactions to the brahmans. Vidura was made the official ceremony treasurer. Duryodhana was assigned to gather the presents the visitors brought. Krishna was tasked with washing the brahmans' feet.

A role should reflect a person's skills and aptitude.

Krishna chose a role that best highlighted his reverence for the great sages. *A servant leader.* Everything went like clockwork. As the sacrifice peaked, Narada *muni*, who was present and observant throughout the sacrifice, smiled as he watched Krishna perform the most mundane tasks on the last day. He decided to stay back to watch the Protector of the Universe carry out his earthly responsibilities as a human.

"O Yudhishthir, please offer *arghya*,[6] to all the kings gathered here today," Bhishma commanded. "When a guru, an officiating priest, a relative, a *snataka*, or a friend stays with you for a year, they become deserving of worship, and you must offer an *arghya* as a sign of respect. Thousands of these kings have been with us for more than a year and earned our respect. Choose the one you believe is most deserving of this honor and start your offering of *arghya* with that person."

---

[6] Sacred water

When small people do great things, it is a sign of their greatness. When great people do small things, it signifies their sweetness.

Grandfather Bhishma's advice felt burdensome to Yudhishthir. "How can I choose from among luminaries much more experienced and knowledgeable than me? It is impossible for me to make that decision. I do not want to be impudent and make the decision. Grandfather, why don't you choose the person I should start with?"

"Krishna." Bhishma did not have to think twice. "He is the most important person in the world. His radiance, power, and brilliance outshine everyone else's. His mere presence lights up this entire ceremony."

Yudhishthir smiled and signaled Sahadeva. Approaching Krishna with a silver platter in one hand and a bowl with a silver spoon containing the sacred *arghya* water in the other, Sahadeva made his offering. Krishna was all set and smiling to accept the Pandavas' worship. Everyone in the audience smiled—all except one.

Jealous Jabbers

Shishupala, the king of Chedi, stood up and smashed a vessel next to him with his foot. The disruption shifted all eyes from Krishna toward the noise.

"Unbelievable! The Pandavas are so immature. The sons of

Pandu have no understanding of the nuances of dharma. Fools seeking counsel from another fool, the son of a river. Worse still, the son of the river defies all moral precepts and offers advice the foolish children blindly follow. A man who offers advice just to make others happy is unworthy. How can a man who is not king be considered worthy of worship? If you think he is worthy by being the eldest, then why not worship his father, Vasudeva? Worshipping a son in front of his father? If you think he is supportive, then why not worship Drupada, a friend and ally? Why not Dronacharya, the guru of the Pandavas? Why not Vyas? Why worship Krishna when the grand old sire Bhishma is here? If you think Krishna is knowledgeable, then why not Ashwatthama? Why bow down to Krishna when Duryodhana is around? Why worship him at the cost of luminaries like Bhishmaka, Paundraka, Rukmi, Ekalavya, Shalya, and the great Karna?" Shishupala's words spewed venom.

An envious person is too busy picking others' faults to count their own blessings; too busy carving others' shortcomings to carve their own destiny.

"If worshiping Krishna was the goal, then why bother inviting everyone? We did not come here to be humiliated. Neither fear nor temptation has drawn us here. Yudhishthir, we came here because we believed you were a virtuous man who wanted to do good in this world. You no longer have our respect because you are worshipping Krishna over everyone else who is worthy. Krishna is unrighteous; he cheated to have Jarasandha killed. Righteousness will leave this courtroom the moment you worship him. Krishna has quietly accepted the offering just as a dog slyly licks the ghee meant for sacrifice. Krishna is completely unworthy of such reverence. Today, the true nature of Yudhishthir, Bhishma, and Krishna was revealed—all pathetic and lowly." Shishupala stormed out of the hall.

The more the filth spewed, the deeper the envy.

Yudhishthir hurried after the angry guest to calm him down and win him back. "All this hatred is hurtful and hateful. It was completely wrong to speak ill of the great Bhishma. Many kings who are much older endorse this honor for Krishna. Would it be possible to be a little more open-minded about this?"

Bhishma stood up and made a daring proclamation, seeing the tender-hearted Yudhishthir struggle against cunning people. "Krishna is the oldest person in the universe. The one opposing the worship of Krishna does not deserve any kindness."

It takes courage to be soft; it takes clarity to be bold.

"Yudhishthir, trying to placate this cunning man is a waste. This assembly has no monarch Krishna has not vanquished. Every celestial being should bow down to him, not just the world's monarchs. In fact, everything in the cosmos revolves around him. So, we ought to honor Krishna alone. There is none older or better than him. I have spoken to men who are both intelligent and experienced. They have recounted many of Krishna's miraculous feats since he was a little boy. Rather than being a random act of devotion, our decision to worship Krishna comes from extensive research and introspection. We do not worship him with hopes of receiving something in return. Just because he is a relative does not mean we must worship him. Our research into deserving male deities led us to believe that none other than Hari is worthy of worship. When it comes to brahmans, Krishna knows more than anyone else. When it comes to the Vedas and the Vedangas, no one is as knowledgeable as Krishna. Krishna is the strongest kshatriya. Nothing a man can do compares to Keshava's powers. Krishna is the wealthiest vaishya and the oldest shudra."

"Broadminded, intelligent, brave, humble, successful, attractive, determined and content—Krishna is abundant in these qualities. He deserves all the adoration we show him because he is our guru and our father. He is the source of everything, and everything eventually dissolves into him. Just as Agnihotra is the best among Vedic rites, the Gayatri the best among meters, the king is best among men, the ocean best among rivers, the moon best among constellations, the sun most luminous, Meru the best among mountains, and Garuda the best among birds, Krishna reigns supreme in all three realms. Remember, this Shishupala is just a baby. His naïve statements reflect his inability to grasp the enormity of Krishna. Who in the three realms would not worship Krishna?"

The grandsire Bhishma's passionate defense inspired

Sahadeva to speak up. "If a monarch who cannot tolerate devotion to Krishna is among us, I will crush his head with my foot!" Glaring at everyone in that assembly, his foot lifted, Sahadeva openly challenged everyone. None said anything. As if to bolster his belief, the sky showered Sahadeva with flowers. A voice proclaimed, "Great!" "Excellent!" The assembly echoed.

Narada spoke his mind. "Even though they are still physically present, men who refuse to worship the lotus-eyed Krishna are spiritually dead. None should talk to such men."

Sahadeva turned confidently toward Krishna and offered him the *arghya* to complete the *yagna*. His wrath exploding from his bloodshot eyes, Shishupala asked, "Which of you will support me and fight against this foolishness? As long as I am here, I will not pander to the Vrishnis' and the Pandavas' capricious desires."

A handful of kings huddled together, clenching their fists and staring down at those who refused to take their side. Concerned, Yudhishthir turned to his grandfather as he watched them band together to cause trouble. Violence was the last thing he wanted during this solemn sacrifice. Bhishma seemed indifferent. Yudhishthir was willing to forsake all for peace, Bhishma was willing to do all to stay assertive.

Bhishma smirked. "O King! Do not be perturbed. Can a dog kill a lion? Dogs bark when lions sleep. For as long as Krishna lies low like the sleeping lion, Shishupala and his followers are fooled into thinking they are the real deal. However, this foolish man's actions will bring about the downfall of these monarchs. The collective wisdom of these rulers has deteriorated."

Krishna was unconcerned by Shishupala's foolishness. When Shishupala overheard the older men arguing, he became furious.

Shishupala's darkness surfaced. He unleashed a torrent of hate speech toward everyone in his vicinity. "You are the legendary wretch of the Kuru clan. Your advice is just as incomplete as your own life. With you in charge, it's the blind leading the blind. Your counsel is the counsel of doom. Your glorification of Krishna, who is unworthy of our praise, has been painful. You arrogant fool, why did your tongue not split into a hundred pieces when you glorified Krishna? You are praising Krishna, the same one whose wicked acts everyone knows. This is so unlike someone supposedly knowledgeable and intelligent."

"What is so significant about his killing a vulture in his childhood? About breaking a wooden cart? About gorging on food when playing with his friend on a mountain? How do you appreciate the one who killed Kamsa at whose home he was a guest and had had meals? Or the one who killed a woman and a cow? How do you worship someone so *adharmic*? Old men like you have bestowed him with the title of Lord of the Universe, but knowing this is untrue, why does Krishna believe you? The supposedly wise Bhishma, you are wicked and clueless about the nature of genuine dharma. You abducted Amba, a woman whose heart had already been broken. Even your brother Vichitravirya was honorable enough not to touch her, knowing that she belonged to another man. But you are obnoxious. If you were a real man, would you possibly allow another man to impregnate your brother's wives? Your vow of celibacy is a farce to hide your incompetence or ignorance. You speak of strong moral principles, but you do not follow these. All your merits come to naught because you have not fathered any son. Your moral compass is off, you have no children, and you are getting on in years. A member of your own family is sure to kill you. Let me tell you of a swan that was like you."

"The swan lived on the shore of a vast ocean. He wanted to make an easy living. He found a new bird quarters and began hovering there lecturing the birds on morality. Even though he did not believe in high moral principles, he encouraged the birds to live by them. He was an inspiration to the birds, and they all pitched in to feed and tend to him. All these birds began to trust him completely very quickly. They had such confidence in him that they left their eggs with him the next time they went hunting. The horrible swan devoured those eggs. The birds would return home each day to discover inexplicably fewer eggs. Yet they never doubted the swan's impeccable moral character. One day, a suspicious bird followed him and caught him in the act. On knowing the truth, the birds ganged up against the swan and slaughtered him. You are like that swan, Bhishma. You do not practice what you preach. When these kings become enraged, you will meet the same fate as the old swan."

Your actions and words should reflect your values.

"Your tall tales about the cowardly trickster Krishna are embarrassing. Along with Arjuna and Bhima, he disguised himself as a brahman and leaped over the wall into Jarasandha's city. He revealed his identity only when the devout Jarasandha was about to wash his feet. Why would the Lord of the Universe mislead the Pandavas and steer them away from the path of dharma? Just as Krishna leads them astray with his deeds, you lead people astray from dharma with your counsel."

Lap of Death

As Bhima listened to Shishupala's incoherent speech, he felt his temper rising. He wanted to confront him and smack him in the face until he passed out from all the profanity. His angry eyes changed into a fierce hue; his wide forehead furrowed in three parallel lines resembling the Ganga's three tributaries. Bhima began gnashing his teeth. *The face of death. Terrifying.* When Bhishma noticed Bhima preparing to attack Shishupala, he rushed over and held down his enormous shoulder. Pacified, Bhima settled.

Fleeting anger is an insanity that can ruin life in an instant. A little support can save the day.

As Shishupala watched Bhishma restrain Bhima, a devious grin spread across his face. He told Bhishma, "Release the giant so that the world can witness him burn down by his power." Instead of being enraged, Bhishma smiled. That grin baffled Shishupala. Bhishma then turned to the whole congregation and declared, "It is my turn to tell a story now."

A smile is the most effective weapon against an adversary; it perplexes them. A smile is the best accessory for a friend; it delights them.

All eyes and ears were on Bhishma. "Damaghosha, the king of Chedi, and his wife, Srutashrava, bore a three-eyed four-limbed baby with an appearance so strange that even they were frightened. The infant brayed instead of crying. Everyone in the kingdom was convinced this birth was ominous. They decided to abandon the child in the woods. A voice, however, intervened and comforted them. 'This child will grow up to be powerful and fortunate. He will not die soon. The one who will kill him has actually been born as well.' The prophecy of the heavenly voice confused the parents. *Should we feel happy or sad? Is this a blessing or a curse?* The mother's anxiety over her child's future made her heart tremble. 'Who will take my child's life?' 'He will visit you soon,' the voice replied. That news shocked the parents. 'Your child's third eye and additional arms will vanish when someone holds him in his lap. That someone will be the one.' The phantom voice said this and vanished."

"From then on, hundreds of other kings called on the king of Chedi. And, whenever a guest arrived, the king would gently put his little one in their lap. King after king cradled the infant, but the prophecy never came true. Just when the parents had almost forgotten the prophecy, Srutashrava's nephews Krishna and Balaram paid them a visit. She was thrilled to see her brother Vasudeva's sons. She held out the infant for them to hold. The child's third eye and extra arms fell off as soon as the baby was in Krishna's lap. The queen froze. She fell at Krishna's feet, begging for mercy. Krishna comforted his distraught aunt. 'I will do as you say, Aunty, and not harm your son.'

'Spare his life, and forgive the one grave mistake he makes. That's all I want of you.'

'I assure you; I will forgive a hundred of Shishupala's serious transgressions, not just one or two. I will consider punishing him only after I have pardoned him for one hundred serious offenses he commits, each of which warrants death.' This is a story about Shishupala. This is also a story about Krishna's magnanimity."

Shishupala lost control of his wrath. His story had been exposed in public. Livid and mouthing profanities, he challenged Krishna to a duel.

Behind every unruly behavior lies a story. While the behavior is there for all to see, the story remains unseen.

Krishna was motionless and attentive through all the narrations and outbursts. Finally, he spoke in a soothing, low voice—no rage nor agitation. "This man, born of a woman of the Satvata race, is the worst enemy of humankind. No one intended to hurt him, yet he has harmed everyone in multiple ways. He is my cousin, my aunt's son, but he once burned down Dwaraka while I was on my way to Pragjyotisha. He launched a guerilla attack and chained all of King Bhoja's servants, when the king was away on vacation in the Raivataka mountain. He stole my father's horse from the sacrificial zone just to disrupt the horse sacrifice ceremony. He abducted the saintly Akrura's wife during her journey from Dwaraka to Sauvira. My sole motivation for patiently enduring all his sins has solely been my solemn vow to my aunt. His desire to possess Rukmini was also completely unwarranted. She did not approve of him either, yet he dared to desire her anyway. O kings, you are all witnesses to his animosity towards my family and me. For all his crimes, he deserves to die."

Shishupala broke into an insane fit of laughter. Clutching his stomach, he began mocking Krishna. "You are so shameless! Discussing your wife's affair with another man in front of the whole court?"

All relationships should have boundaries. Crossing that boundary will result in the disk of time severing the relationship. Tolerance thresholds may vary from person to person—some people hold out longer; some snap sooner—but it is never right to take for granted someone's tolerance.

As Shishupala's raucous laughter echoed through the courtroom, Krishna shut his eyes, wrath swelling inside him. He slowly lifted his index finger only for a dazzling golden disk to spin on it. The Sudharshana *chakra* had materialized, rotating at lightning speed, gearing up for the next moment. "O kings, I had promised his mother I would forgive one hundred of his crimes," Krishna roared. "His time is up. He must perish now."

The Sudharshana *chakra* did its bidding.

Shishupala's body lay lifeless on the courtroom floor, his bloodied head still rolling until it stopped at Bhishma's feet. Suddenly, a brilliant spark emerged from Shishupala's body, soaring toward Krishna and disappearing into his body. *Unbelievable!* Most people were clueless about what happened. But the wise who knew and were thankful to have been allowed to witness this divine phenomenon bowed in reverence.

A good teacher is both strict and forgiving.

Whispers in the courtroom all had praise for Krishna. *He is so quick to forgive the one who was so bitter toward him! His kindness! His benevolence!*

Nobody dared interfere with the sacrifice. Until the successful completion of the Rajasuya sacrifice, with his Sudarshana *chakra*, Sharanga bow, and Kaumodaki *gada*, Krishna stood guard next to Yudhishthir.

Standing Strong in Love

While most people think falling in love is important, Krishna thinks standing in love is more important. He never wavered in his support of the people he cared about and always helped them reach their full potential.

One measure of a great person is how well they handle life's inevitable curveballs. Every situation in life warrants an extraordinary yet appropriate response. Krishna reacted differently to different scenarios. We, too, are shaped by our experiences that determine our reactions to adversity. Sometimes, being modest works, and sometimes, it is best to be bold. Others perceive our personality as a delightful blend of greatness and sweetness when we deliver the correct response.

5

THE INDEFATIGABLE ONE

5.93.6

धर्मकार्यं यतञ्छक्त्या नो चेत्प्राप्नोति मानवः ।
प्राप्तो भवति तत्पुण्यमत्र मे नास्ति संशयः ॥

Dharmakaaryam yatanchbhaktyaa no chetpraapnoti maanavah
Praapto bhavati tatpunyamatra me naasti sanshayah

"If someone gives their best effort to do good but does not succeed, there is no doubt that the merit is still earned."

Sever the ignorant doubt in your heart with the sword of self-knowledge. Observe your discipline. Arise. Stand up. Take action.

Hasty Vow, Sleepless Night, Prophetic Dream

Krishna, the master of *yoga nidra*—the science of mystic slumber—was tossing and turning in bed. Sleep should not ever elude Krishna. Yet he was struggling to catch a wink.

Why was Arjuna so rash? His oath has put the entire war at stake. Yudhishthir gambles before the war; Arjuna gambles during it. These brothers! How can Arjuna kill Jayadratha before sunset? It will be the end of him if he cannot. Those Kauravas will use their entire force and give their all to protect Jayadratha. Can he slice through such a massive army and reach Jayadratha before sunset? How will he do in one day what none could in fourteen days? It is dakshinayana[7] *now, and the sun will set sooner.*

Arjuna's hasty vow was running in a loop in Krishna's head. *My devotee will never perish. He is my devotee. I must protect him and make sure he lives.*

Daruka received a call well past midnight. This was a first—his master, who lived a very balanced and structured life, had never called for work during rest time. So, he rushed into Krishna's tent only to find his master walking back and forth, the worry lines on his forehead fluctuating with each move.

"Ah, Daruka, did you hear about Arjuna's vow? Do you know how far the Kauravas will go to protect Jayadratha? You know I love Arjuna dearly, perhaps much more than I love my sons, wives, relatives, or my other friends. If he fails to keep his commitment and perishes, living on this earth without

---

[7] winter solstice

him will become impossible. I might have to break my own vow and engage in battle tomorrow to help Arjuna keep his. I need to protect my dearest friend. The world will see my fury tomorrow and how much I love the Pandavas. Their friends are my friends, and their enemies are my enemies. Krishna and Arjuna are inseparable. Daruka, I called you to prepare my chariot for tomorrow's onslaught. Place all my shakti weapons, including my most formidable ones—the Sudarshana *chakra*,[8] the Kaumodaki *gada*,[9] the Saranga *dhanush*[10]—on the chariot ready for launch. Yoke my best horses, Shaibya, Valaahaka, Meghapushpa, and Sugriva. Armor them and armor yourself Daruka. The moment I blow my Panchajanya *shankha*[11] in the Rishabha *swara*,[12] you must know it's an emergency and come to me with the chariot immediately. Jayadratha must die by sundown tomorrow."

Once he had briefed Daruka and was sure his charioteer knew his responsibilities, Krishna drifted into a deep slumber. As the chaos settled in Krishna's tent, in another tent, Arjuna found himself falling asleep without much trouble, even though he had lost his son, Abhimanyu, earlier that day. It was not really the best of naps, yet it was one where he could clearly feel Krishna's constant comforting presence by his side. He could not quite tell if he was in the dream state or awake.

Arjuna could *see* Krishna, *hear* his voice, and *feel* his caress. "You have great powers, Arjuna. Remember the Pashupata

---

[8] discus

[9] mace

[10] bow

[11] conch

[12] musical note

astra,[13] the one Lord Shiva gifted you. Use that to eliminate Jayadratha." Arjuna's slumbering mind wandered to reflect on Lord Shiva. The next instant, he felt Krishna holding his hands and flying off rapidly toward the sky. They flew north until they reached the snowy abode of Lord Shiva. The Lord of Destruction greeted them with a smile. "What is your desire?" Shiva asked. "The Pashupata *astra*!" Arjuna wasted no time with his reply. He was also quick to notice next to Shiva the same type and number of flowers he had offered Krishna the previous day. *How did they reach here?* The enigmatic connection between Krishna and Lord Shiva intrigued him. "I have deposited my bow and infallible arrow in the Lake of Nectar. Fetch them and destroy your enemies." Shiva's instructions were clear and direct.

Along with Lord Shiva's associates, Krishna and Arjuna reached the Lake of Nectar. A deadly, thousand-hooded serpent surfaced, spitting fire from all its mouths. Right next to it was another smaller venomous serpent. The two friends closed their eyes, folded their palms, and began chanting the Maharudra mantras. They opened their eyes to find a large bow and arrow instead of the two serpents. As they lifted these and bowed, a young monk with red eyes and blue-black hair emerged from Lord Shiva's body. He then took the bow and arrow from Arjuna's hands and began demonstrating how to use the weapon. As Arjuna started to learn the incantations needed to invoke the Pashupata *astra*, he felt a sense of deep gratitude and rejuvenation. Once the monk had taught Arjuna everything about the super weapon, he flung the bow and arrow back into the lake and vanished. Arjuna bowed again in deep reverence

---

[13] weapon

to Lord Shiva and drifted back to sleep. *A dream is more real than reality.* Arjuna felt more confident now.

Every dream is a reflection of reality, and every reality is a manifestation of a dream.

Destruction and Protection

It was the fourteenth day of the war. The Pandava camp was bustling since the break of dawn. Arjuna and Krishna looked ethereal and indefatigable. The Pandava warriors stood in columns, all set to attack. Krishna spoke: "Today, we have two goals—destroy Jayadratha and protect Yudhishthir. Arjuna will keep his promise of eliminating Jayadratha. Satyaki, Arjuna's disciple, will protect Yudhishthir from becoming Dronacharya's captive."

A goal defined is a goal attained.

Krishna and Arjuna's golden chariot pierced through the Suchimukha *vyuha*[14] that Dronacharya had created to protect Jayadratha. As he watched the shimmery chariot speed toward

---

[14] formation

him, Jayadratha's heart shrunk with terror. He was deep inside the safety net the Kauravas had spun around him, but his heart pounded with every rattle of Arjuna's chariot echoing through the battlefield.

Arjuna's golden armor and the brilliant Gandiva bow dazzled in the morning sun. His formidable face spelled doom for his enemy. *He looks like Yama himself.* A similar thought ran across everyone who saw him whizz past. Then, as if to declare his intent for total annihilation, Arjuna blew Devadatta, his *shankha*. Krishna joined in with the Panchajanya. The chorus of the *shankha*s struck fear into the heart of every Kaurava soldier. Hearts had punctured even before the battle had begun.

A heart filled with fear is a prison.

Arjuna remembered his dream from the previous night. He felt that surge of confidence again. As he went on a rampage, heads began to roll. His arrows sped past right through their targets faster than a blink of an eye. All anyone saw were severed heads dropping down at the speed of light. It was almost as if the twang of the Gandiva bow, the reverberations from its release, and the whooshing of arrows were all part of a symphony in synchrony with the scream of dying men. *This must be the dance of death.* Everyone was in a state of shock.

Every emotion in life has music. Feeling the rhythm of life is about staying attuned to each emotion.

Dumarshana's regiment could not check Arjuna's onslaught. Dushasana's elephants could not trample Arjuna's might. Razing armies to the ground, pulverizing their weapons, and crushing their confidence, Arjuna reached the periphery of the Padma *vyuha* guarded by the great Dronacharya.

"Acharya, please give me way and allow me to reach Jayadratha so that I can fulfill my vow." Arjuna was at his politest when talking to his teacher, but Dronacharya stood there fixed like a rock.

Arjuna had no choice but to fight his teacher. He knew Dronacharya had conspired to have his son killed, but he had undying respect for his teacher. Yet, this was responsibility over respect. He could not let respect come in the way of fulfilling his duties. This was an equal battle—the teacher and student anticipating each other's every move. Neither was willing to back down. Krishna stepped in. Sounding a warning to Arjuna, he said. "This is just a distraction. Forget everything about killing Jayadratha now. If you drag this thing with your guru, let me tell you, your vow will remain unfulfilled."[15]

---

[15] Krishna wanted Arjuna to continue loving Dronacharya for being his teacher and the knowledge he gained from him, but he also wanted him to disagree with his guru for his wrongdoings.

Love and discipline must co-exist in every relationship. Love should not make one too flexible, and discipline should not make one too rigid.

Arjuna realized Krishna was right, so he diverted his attention from his guru. Arjuna's chariot rose and circled above Dronacharya as a mark of respect before whizzing past him toward the *vyuha*. Arjuna's sudden change of plans left Dronacharya seething. He hollered. "Arjuna, are you fleeing out of fear?" Arjuna turned and smiled. "You are my teacher, not my enemy right now. I am your disciple and like your son. My actions cannot upset you as it would not a father or a teacher. Besides, I do not know anyone in this whole wide world who can outwit you in a battle." Before Dronacharya could respond, his disciple's chariot had gone so far away that it seemed like a speck. His ploy to distract Arjuna had failed.

When you say no to something important, say yes to something more substantial.

Krishna and Arjuna had to make up for lost time. As they were speeding toward the center of the *vyuha* protecting Jayadratha, their chariot was suddenly stopped. In front of them stood a mighty warrior who seemed to have appeared out of thin air. Srutayudha, the mace warrior, was blocking their path. Blessed with an invincible mace that the god of water Varuna had gifted him, this king was famous for his sudden and torturous assaults. As was his reputation, he wasted no time harassing Krishna and Arjuna.

Srutayudha was blessed with the boon that would allow him to remain undefeated in combat for as long as he had his mace with him. But, as with all boons, this too came with a warning: If he attacks anyone weaponless, his mace will boomerang and destroy him.

Arjuna felt utterly defenseless against the onslaught of this speed maniac. Rage so consumed Srutayudha that he began charging recklessly. He did not realize that his mace had flown out of his hand and hit the weaponless Krishna. Within moments, the mace bounced off Krishna's unscathed shoulder, veered around, and began charging toward Srutayudha. It was too late by the time he realized his mistake. The mace smashed his head, and the mace warrior dropped dead. Srutayudha's stupidity had ended the fight too soon, leaving Arjuna free to continue his onslaught, much to the shock of the Kaurava army.

Destiny boomerangs: the filth you hurl at others comes around with higher intensity.

Arjuna's chariot left a trail of corpses, forcing the Kaurava soldiers to either make way for, or stay far away from the chariot. As the sun raced to the western horizon, challenging Arjuna's fleeting chariot, Krishna tugged at the reigns to nudge the horses to go faster. A drop of water splashed on Krishna's soft and sensitive skin. He leaned over to take a closer look at the horses. They were in pain and tears. Krishna could see the exhaustion, the intense strain of the rough day, the thirsty mouths, and the lacerations across their body from the embedded arrows. Their energy sucked dry, the horses could go no faster, no matter how much they tried.

Krishna turned to look at Arjuna. "What should we do now, Krishna?" "The horses need rest and rejuvenation." Arjuna quickly hopped off the chariot. He let Krishna care for the horses as he continued his fight on foot. With no chariot for help, Arjuna soldiered on unabated. He even had a hint of a smile on his face.

The Kauravas saw this as an opportunity. They surrounded him just as they had trapped Abhimanyu the previous day. But then they soon realized that Arjuna, without a chariot, was even more dangerous. Arjuna was immersed in combat when Krishna came rushing. "The horses have no water to drink."

"There is water! Turn around and see for yourself."[16]

Don't depend on resources; depend on resourcefulness.

---

[16] Most people give up when they don't have sufficient resources. When we anchor our lives to one limitation, we make ourselves helpless. Instead of centering everything on that helplessness, put in some effort and try to overcome it by focusing on things that do not limit you. Destiny may hand out shortcomings and limits, but it is up to the human mind to overcome these boundaries and become limitless.

Krishna turned around to find an arrow drilling into the ground. Suddenly, a fresh fountain of water gushed from the center of the battlefield. Arjuna had addressed Krishna's concern before he could explain the problem. The fountain turned into a puddle, then a pond, and soon it became a freshwater lake to which birds flocked from everywhere. While he was demolishing his enemy, Arjuna had also created a canopy and a wall of arrows to shield Krishna and the horses from the enemy.

Krishna smiled and led the horses toward the water. Tending to their wounds and whispering comforting words into their ears, Krishna pulled out arrows from their bodies. He massaged their exhausted bodies and fed them fodder. Allies and enemies were amazed as they watched Krishna and Arjuna. Unfazed by the bloody war surrounding him, Krishna was absorbed in caring for the horses. *So reminiscent of the flute-playing Krishna with his cows in the groves of Vrindavan.* Onlookers could not help but feel transported to the Govardhana Hills.

Krishna's care rid the horses of all fatigue. Soon, as they felt rejuvenated, Krishna yoked the horses to the chariot and brought it to Arjuna. The sun was about to set, yet the two friends appeared calm. Their faces did not reflect any burden of the battle as they went about their duties with a smile. They loved doing what they did.

Dharma has five bases, each bringing stability to different life aspects.

1. *Jnana* or knowledge stabilizes intelligence.
2. *Prema* or love stabilizes the heart.
3. *Nyaya* or justice stabilizes the *atma* or soul.

4. *Tyaga* or sacrifice stabilizes the urges of the body.
5. *Dhairya* or patience stabilizes the mind.

Stability in all these aspects fills one with compassion, and that compassion is *dharma*. One who has *dharma* is sensitive toward the pain of others.

Krishna embodied stability in these five aspects and showed compassion in the unlikeliest situations and ways not ordinarily possible.

Duryodhana was bothered by the progress Krishna and Arjuna had made. He approached his teacher, Dronacharya, with a barrage of complaints and criticisms. Dronacharya tried to explain, but Duryodhana would have none of it. "You are not trying hard enough!" Dronacharya eventually relented. "Yes, I am too old to combat Arjuna. Your age and power match. How about battling him yourself?"

"What are you saying? How would I stand a chance against the expert bowman when the most powerful warriors of this universe, including you, failed to stop him?" Dronacharya's decision to back down shocked him.

Dronacharya tried to allay Duryodhana's concerns. "You are as dear to me as my son Ashwatthama. So, I will offer you a special gift that will make you invincible. You can defy even the gods. I will secure your torso with this impenetrable armor blessed by Lord Brahma. Yes, this is the same armor that protected Indra during his fight with Vritrasura."

On birthing a pearl, the oyster dies.
On birthing fruit, the flower dies.

The same holds true for teachers and parents
who do not set their dependents free on time.

Their dependents will become the cause
of their ruin.

Duryodhana felt strong and confident as Dronacharya put the armor on him. Once ready, the Kaurava prince rushed to the battlefield to block Arjuna from reaching Jayadratha. On seeing a determined Duryodhana, Krishna spoke to Arjuna. "The Kaurava lord himself is out to challenge you. Do not underestimate him. His arrows are powerful and can travel great distances. He seems all set to prove that he is formidable in a fight. He has been raised in comfort and luxury. He also has grown up hating the Pandavas. Right now, he is extremely angry and desperate to stop your progress. Remember, a desperate fighter is tenfold harder to defeat. Arjuna, he is the cause of all your pain and suffering. Let him know pain and suffering. Let him know what it means to challenge you."

Even before Arjuna could launch his attack, Duryodhana's arrows were speed raining on him, giving Arjuna barely a moment to nock the arrows on his bow. Duryodhana's target was not Arjuna alone; he was attacking Krishna, too. Each of Arjuna's efforts went in vain because he just could not counter the Kaurava king. His arrows seemed useless and powerless against Duryodhana. Observing the lopsided fight, Krishna was livid with Arjuna. "What do I see? Your arrows are bouncing off Duryodhana, but his arrows are piercing through my body. It is agonizing to have all those arrows penetrate my flesh. I have never experienced such severe agony. At this point, he seems to be a better fighter than you, or you have lost your skills. It is almost sundown, and fate is against us today. How else do you explain this, if, of all people, Duryodhana ends up defeating you? You might as well surrender and proclaim Duryodhana too good for you."

Krishna's gnarly comment had the right effect on Arjuna. He began trembling in anger, but his brain was plotting an attack. "You are taunting me, Krishna. You know well what I can do. All his confidence stems from the special armor he has worn. Just about any arrow cannot penetrate the armor if worn that way. Only my guru and I know that special way of wearing it. All of Duryodhana's courage rests on that borrowed armor. But then he does not seem to know anything about using the armor. He is like a bull carrying a burden, oblivious to its value. I know how to crack this armor. My father, Indra, had taught me. Watch me as I destroy him." [17]

A cackle of hyenas borrows confidence from each other, but a lion derives confidence from its own strength.

---

[17] Duryodhana's confidence came from the borrowed armor, while Arjuna's came from his own abilities.

Just as Arjuna was about to release the powerful Manav *astra*, the arrow split into two. Someone had launched a sudden attack on him from another direction with no warning—quite against the warrior codes. *Ashwatthama?!* The rule breaker was none other than Dronacharya's son. Unperturbed, Arjuna began showering Duryodhana with arrows, explicitly aiming for those parts of his body not shielded by the armor. Suddenly, Duryodhana felt a shooting pain in his fingertip. *Such precision in his aim?* He felt arrow after arrow pierce his palms, fingernails, fingertips, ... Unable to withstand the unbearable torture, Duryodhana fled the battlefield, leaving the Pandava soldiers mocking him.

Even the most powerful have a weak spot that can be spotted on close observation.

Krishna and Arjuna were painfully aware of the sun being so close to dipping into the western horizon. Trying to catch up with time, they began racing toward the Suchimukha *vyuha*. They had to end Jayadratha.

Krishna realized that the endgame hinged on chariot-maneuvering skills. He needed an extra push. So, too, the horses. "Arjuna, drum up some motivation for us with the twangs of the Gandiva bow!" Arjuna drew the strings of the Gandiva. Krishna blew the Panchajanya to harmonize with the loud twang. The thunderous roar of the conch and bow string was just the starting sound Krishna needed to zip faster through enemy lines.

By this time, Yudhishthir sent Satyaki and Bhima to help Arjuna in his impossible mission. Satyaki had to fight tooth and nail on his way to meet Arjuna. He exhausted his final ounce of energy when he fought with Bhoorishravas. During the battle, he lost his chariot and had to fight on his feet. When Krishna spotted Satyaki hobbling, he blew the Panchajanya in the Rishabha *swara*, and in that instant, Daruka appeared. Krishna signaled Satyaki to hop onto his chariot and use it. With Satyaki and Bhima on either side, Arjuna charged into the *vyuha* with renewed vigor. Every single Kaurava leader was trying to stall Arjuna's entry into *vyuha*. All eyes flitted between Arjuna and the rapidly setting sun. *If only we could keep him away until sunset!* Krishna saw through their plan and knew it was nearly impossible for Arjuna to push past these soldiers and reach Jayadratha before sunset. This needed some serious thinking.

Not every fight is won with might alone. Some fights need wit. Where brawn ends, the brain must begin.

Implicit Trust

Before taking any step, Krishna wanted to confirm something. "Arjuna, do you trust me implicitly? Will you do as I say without batting an eyelid?"

"Of course!" Arjuna looked at Krishna, waiting eagerly to

absorb his friend's instructions. "When I signal, simply shoot." Arjuna knew what he had to do.

Faith is not the absence of fear. It means stepping on fear's head and walking the path drawn by God.

Just then, the sun unexpectedly and swiftly sank into the horizon. *What just happened?! How did the sun disappear in a fraction of a second?* The loud celebratory roar of the Kaurava army boomed through the darkness. Everyone rushed toward Jayadratha. *He has survived*! Arjuna's spirit sank with the sun. Just Jayadratha looked up at the sky.

"SHOOT!" Krishna's voice thundered across the battlefield.

In a split second, the infallible Pashupata *astra* zipped toward Jayadratha, pierced right through his head, and lifted it high up in the sky.

Eyes popped out of sockets, and they were all now on the arrow embedded with the head as it soared into the sky. Suddenly, to the dismay of everyone there, the sun shone brilliantly behind the flying head. The sun had not set yet! The Sudarshana chakra of Krishna had covered the sun in such a way that it was invisible for a few moments.

While believers can see God's marvels every day, nonbelievers will have to wait for science to explain it to them.

Krishna instructed Arjuna to make his *astra* move with the head toward Jayadratha's father, who was performing his evening prayers near Samantapanchaka, at the far end of the battlefield. Arjuna did so. The *astra* shot ahead with Jayadratha's chopped head toward Samantapanchaka and disappeared after placing the chopped head of the son on the father's lap. As he felt something drop onto his lap, the father jumped up with a start and inadvertently dropped his son's head to the ground. The moment Jayadratha's head fell to the ground, his father's head exploded into a thousand pieces. With Jayadratha's passing, the sun shone bright for a few moments before sliding into the horizon.

The Kauravas let out a wail of loss—they were this close to victory. But Krishna and Arjuna had robbed them of it. They walked away silently, heads hanging low from the shame of being unable to save their friend who had trusted them with his life. Krishna hopped out of the chariot and ran arms open toward Arjuna to hug him. Arjuna fell at Krishna's feet. "You are the reason for this victory." Krishna showed Arjuna the battlefield and declared: In just one day, you and Satyaki have destroyed seven Kaurava *akshauhinis*." The boom of conches declared Arjuna's incredible victory.

As they returned to camp, Arjuna wondered why Krishna made him throw Jayadratha's head in his father's lap. Krishna told the intriguing story of Jayadratha's father with a smile. "It took a lot for Brihatkshatra to father Jayadratha. All that austerity and asceticism led to him being blessed with a son whom regular men could never kill. Jayadratha could die only at the hands of the finest heroes and with the most powerful of weapons. The boon rendered his son immortal. Almost. He felt the boon was not all that foolproof. So, he requested another favor—that the head of the person who drops his son's head on the ground explode into a thousand pieces. With this boon too granted, Brihatkshatra now believed his son was immortal. Arjuna, even if you had cut off Jayadratha's head before sunset, your head would have exploded too, as soon as you would have dropped his head to the ground. I asked you to throw Jayadratha's head into his father's lap so he would be blamed for dropping it and would suffer from his own boon.

Parents often neglect character when building a child's future.[18]

Arjuna was in awe of Krishna's wisdom. Unlike him, who was tunnel-visioned, Krishna saw problems in their entirety and evaluated everything before solving them. *I feel so lucky Krishna protects me from every direction.*

Peace at last! Krishna inhaled the fresh air of victory and calm as the chariot raced to camp.

Multidimensional thinkers listen intently, observe keenly, understand, think differently, and act wisely.

---

[18] Brihatkshatra focused on boons to protect his child's future but neglected character development. If Jayadratha had greater character, he would not have needed the boons and would have lived fully. While cutting corners, the father cut short the son's life.

6

THE MASTER STRATEGIST

7.181.29–30

धर्मसंस्थापनार्थं हि प्रतिज्ञैषा ममाव्यया।
ब्रह्म सत्यं दमः शौचं धर्मो ह्रीः श्रीधृतिः क्षमा।
यत्र तत्र रमे नित्यमहं सत्येन ते शपे ॥

Dharmasamsthaapanaartham hi pratignaisha mamaavyayaa
Brahma satyam damah shaucham hreeh shreedhritih kshama
Yatra tatra rame nityamaham satyena te shape

"I am committed to upholding dharma, truth, discipline, purity, righteousness, humility, patience, and forgiveness. No matter where I am, I will stay true to myself."

The door to life's potential swings open or shut depending on our decisions.

Deadlock

The fourteenth day of the war was the most perilous. None could have predicted any of the unexpected turns they saw that day. The day was just as uneventful as the night was enthralling. Arjuna had sworn that day to either kill Jayadratha before nightfall or at least die trying. The Kauravas' hopes had rested heavily on Arjuna's commitment until Krishna's vision derailed it all. Their optimism faded as the sun set over the western sky, and Jayadratha lay dead. As hope dwindled, anger swelled among the ranks.

They felt as though someone was trying to mess with the sunset, but no one could put their finger on it. Defeating Arjuna seemed insurmountable to Duryodhana for the very first time. *Did he not just hack through our seemingly impenetrable army to kill Jayadratha?* To cope with their crushing loss that day, the Kaurava chiefs had disregarded every battle regulation to continue fighting far past dusk.

A master strategist steps away to examine what is near and closely inspects whatever is far—looking at the fine print and the big picture—before making smart judgments, knowing that distance influences people's perspectives.

The two armies fiercely battled against one another as night fell over Kurukshetra. Dronacharya was particularly livid. He had been mercilessly stopped from delivering on his promise to safeguard Jayadratha from Arjuna. King Shivi led an army of assailants to kill Dronacharya; his aim was to obliterate the guru under the cover of darkness. He punctured Dronacharya with thirty deadly arrows and even killed his charioteer.

Seeing his teacher struggle, Duryodhana quickly arranged a substitute chariot for him. Furious, Dronacharya mounted his new chariot and unleashed an unexpected salvo of attacks on King Shivi. Soon, King Shivi's head was flying off, embedded with the arrow released from Dronacharya's bow. Dronacharya did not stop at that. His wrathful blitzkriegs against the Pandava army continued, and it seemed like the dance of death.

Bhima rushed to the battlefield, which had now become Dronacharya's slaughterhouse—his seemingly endless spray of arrows butchering the Pandava army. Just then, seeking to avenge his father's death, the Kalinga king's son attacked Bhima with his army. *Now is not the time!* Bhima had no time for a petty squabble, so he jumped onto the king's chariot and smashed him with his fist, crushing every bone in his body. The prince dropped dead.

As Bhima's frenzied raid exterminated one strong fighter after another, Drumada, one of Duryodhana's brothers, joined the fray. With one strong mace strike, Bhima destroyed his challenger's chariot. But Drumada was quick to leap onto his brother Dushkarna's chariot. Bhima launched himself mercilessly on that chariot—his agility stunning the two brothers. The Kaurava troops fled as they saw Bhima grind the skulls of two completely grown-up men with his palms.

Enraged by the damage the Pandava brothers were causing, Ashwathama went on a killing rampage, slaying many of the

Panchala princes. Duryodhana and Karna, too, joined in the death frenzy. Karna's magnificent display of valor made Duryodhana happy. Hope resurfaced every time he watched his friend's show of unmatched dexterity and talent. Duryodhana maneuvered his chariot closer to Karna's and screamed over the battle sounds. "O Radheya, the river of death is overflowing now. You are my only hope. Build a dam to divert the bitter cold waves of death from sweeping away our troops."

Finding hope in someone else's ability is the same as finding mangoes on a lemon tree.

Karna admired Duryodhana's reliance on him, especially his confidence in his expertise. "Yes, I will fight now. Arjuna's death is certain. The shakti *astra* that Indra gave me will be my weapon of choice. Today, the father will become the cause of his son's death. No one can save him today. And once I am done with him, I will finish the Pandava army. Brother, you will rule the world as long as you have me by your side."

Building dependencies for others means building dependencies for oneself. Leaning can make the weak stronger but the strong weaker.

Kripacharya could not help but reprimand Karna when he heard his boastful banter. "If words could kill, you would end the entire army. You have a lot to say, do you not? But your actions do not match your pretentious words. Did you not treat us to your battle with Arjuna outside the Virata kingdom? How do you expect to hold off the armies of the five Pandavas if you could not stand before one? You are like clouds that thunder but never rain. All this talk holds only as long as Arjuna is nowhere near you. Stand before him, and it is all air. A kshatriya's actions should outshout his words. The world has seen Arjuna's deeds but has only heard of your noisy and hollow boasts. One arrow of Arjuna will puncture them all and jolt you into reality."

Rather than trumpeting your successes, silently bask in your contribution.

The insult was too much for Karna. "The world will watch. I will kill Arjuna for sure with this weapon Indra has given me. As for you, you are an old brahman who is useless in battle. All you do is seek the Pandavas' protection. Speak one more word against me, and I will cut off your tongue."

Karna's words infuriated Ashwathama. He charged toward Karna, brandishing his sword, cautioning him against insulting his uncle. But Duryodhana intercepted him just in time. "Ashwathama, a brahman should not display such rage. Forgive Karna. Let us face the enemy together instead." Even though Duryodhana doused the flames of discontent, Kripa and Ashwathama knew Karna's pride would fall at Arjuna's feet.

An individual agenda is a conflict that separates; a common goal is a fight that unites.[19]

Through the thick, impenetrable darkness, the troops could not tell their own from the enemy's. "TORCHES!" Dronacharya called out. In an instant, millions of torches lit up the battlefield. With torches in hand, the soldiers were mere streetlamps in this battle between stalwarts.

Karna was terrifying that night. Everyone saw him release an amazing succession of arrows. Under the light of the torches, his arrows burned brighter. That evening, he looked undefeatable. Soldiers scooted in all directions, trying to dodge his cruel arrows.

When Arjuna saw the hell Karna had let loose, he turned to Krishna. "Ride my chariot to the other side of the battlefield. He will soon wipe off of our army even before sunrise."

Krishna knew now was not the time to rebel against Karna. He knew Arjuna's talent was not enough to protect him from the shakti *astra* that Karna had. After all, Indra had blessed him with it, and it had never once missed its mark.

Yet, instead of demoralizing Arjuna by telling him what he could not do, Krishna chose to help him set his priorities in order. "I know Karna is wreaking havoc, but your bigger concern should be Dronacharya's vow of capturing Yudhishthir alive. Your pursuit of Karna will leave Yudhishthir unguarded.

---

[19] While the Kauravas were on their ego trips and could barely tolerate each other, elsewhere on the battlefield, the Pandavas were on a mission, working together.

Dronacharya will use this darkness to plot his capture. You know that would end the war, leaving you with no chance to exact revenge. Your most crucial task is defending Yudhishthir. Leave Karna to the one other person powerful enough to stop him, your nephew Ghatotkacha, the son of Bhima.

Pausing is not quitting. Engaging is easy, quitting is easy, but pausing is not. Engaging comes from passion, and quitting from panic, but pausing comes from staying calm. A master strategist knows when to fight and when to fold—never giving up, instead using the pause to gather ammunition to pick up the fight again.

Gigantic Trap

Arjuna begrudgingly accepted Krishna's suggestion. *There is merit in what he is saying. But I could totally take on Karna right now*. Yudhishthir's safety was the priority now. Arjuna shut his eyes and thought of Ghatotkacha.

Instantly standing in front of his chariot was a giant. Ghatotkacha had once told his father, Bhima, "You can just summon me when you think of me. I'll be there, right in front of you." Since then, every time the brothers thought of him, he faithfully showed up the next instant. Krishna grinned at the soft giant. "We need you to use your might right now, great son of Bhima, Ghatotkacha. Darkness is your domain. But look at the battlefield now, it is not favoring the Pandava brothers. Your father and his siblings are fighting for survival. Darkness is engulfing their armies. Karna is tearing through our army. He must be checked right now. Nobody on our side can halt his madness but you. Use your maya[20] techniques and destroy Duryodhana's army. Challenge Karna. Eliminate that reckless one with your divine missiles if you can. Trying to grab the king are Dronacharya and Ashwatthama. Arjuna must guard Yudhishthir from the father–son duo.

Leadership is like gymnastics—precision is key, and errors can be disastrous.

Ghatotkacha was all set for the night. Arjuna assigned Satyaki to help with Ghatotkacha's attack, certain that the two would annihilate the enemies. *What is this? Who is this?* Ghatotkacha's presence alone was terrifying. They had never seen anything like this. As he walked toward the center, the Pandava troops quickly made way for him. He was so ginormous that his foot alone could crush a mini army. The darkness appeared darker.

Ghatotkacha wasted no time and headed straight for Karna. An ocean of fighters aimed all their arrows at Ghatotkacha, hoping to bring him down. But then the arrows were like stubble hair on Ghatotkacha's gigantic body. Brushing them off like dust, he ran through the soldiers, smashing them to pulp,

[20] illusion

and leaving a heap of terribly disfigured bodies. Death trailed him as he ended thousands.

Duryodhana immediately understood the giant's goal and called for his brother. "Dushasana! Move in with a massive army to help Karna in his battle with Ghatotkacha." Just then Jatasura's son, Alambusha, rode up to him with a request. "Bhima had killed my father. I have been waiting for a chance to avenge his death." *Ah! this is God sent!* Duryodhana, not wanting to waste an opportunity, said to Alambusha, "You must make Bhima suffer the same pain you went through when you lost your father. Go and kill his son now!" Like a moth innocuously flying into raging fire, Alambusha raced towards Ghatotkacha.

Underestimating an enemy is overestimating oneself.

The newcomer was brave. Thus far, he was the bravest to face Ghatotkacha, publicly challenging the giant to a fair combat. The clash was violent, bloody, and terrible. It was also even—both rakshasas were adept at maya warcraft. For those watching from the flanks, this battle was spellbinding.

Enough! Now for the end! Ghatotkacha stopped abruptly, having decided he had battled enough. He first leaped high toward the sky and suddenly swooped down, his sword unsheathed, aimed right at Alambusha's neck. The head rolled with one tidy sweep. The great speed and force with which the elimination took place astounded the troops.

Ghatotkacha picked up the severed head from the dusty battlefield, headed toward Duryodhana's chariot, and dropped it at Duryodhana's feet. Staring right into Duryodhana's eyes, he said, "They say one should not visit a king empty-handed. Here, accept my present—your friend's head. Just wait a little longer. I will be back with another head—your dearest friend Radheya's.

Intimidate if you want to win against an adversary; encourage if you want to win over a friend.

The near encounter with the huge rakshasa sent a chill down Duryodhana's spine. He stood there transfixed on his chariot. This threat was real. No missile in his arsenal could damage, let alone destroy, this giant. The soldiers lost the war in their heads when they saw their ruler tremble. *It is useless to even try now.* Most understood by now that their spikes, swords, or arrows were not enough to cause any harm to the giant. *Perhaps Karna can. Isn't he one who is blessed with potent divine weapons from Parashuram and Indra?* With this hope in mind, many soldiers followed the giant to see his duel with Karna.

Ghatotkacha launched his attack using maya techniques. That left thousands of soldiers all around Karna dead. Karna could not save any of them, but he could at least defend himself from all the maya Ghatotkacha was hurling at him. As the night went on, Ghatotkacha's maya energy grew stronger, and Karna's defense became weaker.

One moment Ghatotkacha was pummeling people on earth; the next, he was raining arrows from the heavens. Nobody knew his exact location at any given time—he was that swift and slippery. *This is so incredulous! How can someone so massive move so fast? How can someone change forms so quickly?* The soldiers trembled in terror as they watched the giant assume graphic and horrific shapes.

Karna continued to counter the agile giant's attacks with every weapon in his arsenal. His rare successes at erasing Ghatotkacha's enchantment barely lasted seconds—the giant would devise another trick to test Karna's intelligence.

Knowledge Is Magic

Karna was living a nightmare. Things could not have been worse for him. Finally, a savior—Alayudha, another enormous rakshasa, arrived. Alayudha had previously met Duryodhana with a request. "I am related to Kirmeera and Bakasura. Bhima slayed all of them. I want to..."

Duryodhana understood the drift and was all too happy to let him join the fray. Karna was relieved when Alayudha tore into Ghatotkacha with a thunderous roar. Of course, that was just temporary relief. Alayudha matched Ghatotkacha's size but not his strength. Soon, Ghatotkacha was walking toward Duryodhana's chariot with Alayudha's head, placing it right next to Alambusha's. Ghatotkacha grinned maliciously at Duryodhana and resumed his battle with Karna. *Now, the finale!*

He started fighting Karna with considerably more powerful magical techniques and fresh vigor. When he hurled dark clouds raining fire at Karna, Karna countered those with the *vayavya astra*. When he conjured up clouds with arrows, Karna used the *aindra astra* to make them disappear. But Ghatotkacha, as if he was many armies rolled into one, relentlessly slaughtered hundreds of Kaurava soldiers despite Karna's counterattacks. Chaos and terror reigned among the ranks and files of the Kaurava army. Fearing they would all perish, they begged Karna, "Save us! He will not stop until all of us die. Kill him, please, or else this war is lost! Use your Vasavi shakti. Save us all from certain death. Show us compassion. End this bloody carnage now!"

If followers have to beg for compassion, it is a sign that leadership has failed.

Pressure began mounting on Karna from all directions to use his most powerful and prized weapon. He was left with no choice. He had exhausted every weapon he had against Ghatotkacha, but none worked. He had defeated him twice that night, yet he had reemerged stronger. *Why is fate playing this nasty trick on me? I was saving it to use against Arjuna!*

From the moment he set foot on the battlefield, he had no opportunity to engage with Arjuna directly. They were in different places, battling different people. *It seems fate is on Arjuna's side.*

Indra had foreseen all this. He knew that Arjuna would stay unharmed as long as Krishna was with him. When receiving the weapon and the instructions, Karna did not pay full attention to what Indra had to say. Instead, all his focus was on Vasavi shakti in his hands. "You can use this weapon only once and against only one opponent. The moment you do that, it will return to me!" Karna's mind was elsewhere. *Ha! I just need one chance to use it against Arjuna. All these warnings and requirements are so pointless.* In hindsight, though, as the clamor for using Vasavi shakti against Ghatotkacha became louder, he began to feel the weight of the warnings.

Should life checkmate anyone, the only option is to submit to fate.

As Karna prepared to release Vasavi shakti from his bow, he felt a searing pain in his chest, almost as if his heart were being pierced. *Why am I even here now?* His aim to shatter the gigantic Ghatotkacha was also about to shatter his only dream: killing Arjuna. He had toiled relentlessly for years to realize this sole dream. *So many sacrifices, so many austerities, so much kindness, so much training, so much compromise, for what? To be defeated by fate?* Karna felt helpless. It seemed as if Kunti's desire to protect her son was far stronger than Karna's desire to kill Arjuna. Here he was now, dream crumbling, staring at the giant that had come between him and his dream. *This is Krishna's doing! This gigantic obstruction—his checkmate move!*

Karna knew that the Kauravas would not escape obliteration if he did not use Vasavi shakti. Tears streaming down his cheeks, Karna looked at Duryodhana one last time before releasing the divine missile. "Just know this. The instant I release Vasavi shakti toward Ghatotkacha, it will spell the end of all your fantasies of world domination." He was half expecting him to stop him. But Duryodhana was more focused on ending Ghatotkacha.

Nature's patience always transforms trapped things into something precious—dirt trapped in an oyster transforms into a pearl; a rock trapped inside the earth transforms into a diamond. But humans lack patience, so nothing precious comes from their feeling trapped—insecurity transforms into deep envy, envy transforms into hatred, and hatred transforms into murderous rage.

Even he believes there is no other way. Karna realized the futility of it all. *If we survive the night, we could consider various approaches to destroying the Pandavas. But if we do not, what good are dreams to the dead?* Karna wiped off his tears and finally released the brilliant, powerful, and precise Vasavi shakti toward Ghatotkacha's chest. Like lightning flashing across the dark night, Vasavi shakti zipped at amazing speed and thundered right into the monster's heart.

Ghatotkacha knew it was all over for him. Before dying, though, he wanted just a little more for his father. Defying death for a moment, Ghatotkacha enlarged himself to a size larger than human comprehension and collapsed on the Kaurava army. Thousands of men, elephants, horses, and chariots were crushed under his weight. That one fall destroyed the entire Akshauhini division. Even in death, he had caused the most significant loss to the Kaurava army. Those who escaped death felt intense relief. *We will never have to suffer from his torture or live in constant fear of his next move.*

Everyone falls. But should your fall make you fall in others' eyes or help you rise in their eyes?

Duryodhana rushed up to Karna. To honor him, he welcomed him into his chariot. "Words fall short, Karna. You are the greatest warrior that walked the earth." Turning to the Kaurava soldiers, he said, "Rejoice! Celebrate this victory!" The Kaurava barracks erupted into one big festival. People waved torches as they danced and sang. Karna, of course, was in no mood to celebrate his worst loss—Vasavi shakti had returned to Indra.

Silence fell over the Pandava barracks. Ghatotkacha's loss was personal to the Pandava brothers. Bhima gasped. He saw his brothers wailing, yet he found it hard to believe that his son was no more. *He was supposed to be near immortal, wasn't he? With such astounding abilities, he was supposed to live forever, wasn't he? Wasn't he more powerful than me?* Unable to process this grief, Bhima sat down on the dusty battleground, hitting his forehead with his hands, and crying uncontrollably. Nothing that Yudhishthir said to console him mattered. *This loss will not heal.* Yudhishthir was devastated to see his brother so broken. Ghatotkacha was a favorite child.

Triumph and failure are as fleeting as rice bubbling and water boiling—up now, down next; winner today, loser tomorrow.

Krishna reached the place where Ghatotkacha lay dead. He jumped off the chariot and burst into dance. He did not join the brothers in their grief. His twirls and leaps of joy left everyone dumbstruck. He ran to Arjuna and hugged him repeatedly. *What is this? Joy when everyone is drowning in sorrow?* Arjuna was livid. He found Krishna's behavior inappropriate and incredulous. "Krishna, we are suffering, can you not see? What makes you so happy? Our beloved child is no longer with us. What does this mean?"

Finally, Relief

Krishna gripped Arjuna's shoulders and said, "Today is the happiest day of my life. Radheya is no longer the owner of Vasavi shakti. He has used up the only chance he had to use it. I am at ease now. O Partha, if only you knew of the sleepless nights that I spent thinking about the one in possession of Vasavi shakti. But now the shakti has left. Karna has left as well. As long as he owned that weapon, he was invincible. Until the shakti was with Karna, anyone thinking that you were undefeatable was wrong. When I visited Hastinapur before the battle began, Duryodhana had bragged to me, 'Karna alone is enough for me to wipe out the Pandavas and win the war.' I had seen those smirks on Bhishma's and Dronacharya's faces. They did not want Karna to have such power. But I knew Duryodhana was right. He is self-centered, and his focus on someone implies the person is an invaluable asset. From the moment he saw Karna, Duryodhana instinctively knew that he was superior to everyone, including you, even Arjuna."

Divinity transcends human frailties; where human perspective ends, divine insight begins.

"Bhishma was mistaken when he called Karna an *ardharathi* based on the two curses he had and the loss of his *kavacha* and *kundala*. He had ignored the fact that being in possession of Vasavi shakti made Karna even more powerful than the gods in battle. Can you imagine what would have happened if he had with his *kavacha* and *kundala*, the Vasavi shakti? Not even Indra, Kubera, or Varuna could have confronted him in a war. In the face of Karna's skill, even your Gandiva bow and my Sudarshan *chakra* would have been useless. Lucky for you, Indra removed his *kundala* and *kavacha* to give him Vasavi shakti. With Vasavi shakti no longer in his arsenal, Karna is just a lethal serpent without fangs. He can be defeated now. You alone are enough to counter him at this level. You have never known nor seen Karna's brilliance, but I know. He is as outstanding as Yudhishthir, if not greater. It is easy to destroy Karna now that he has become more human. Right now, I am just overjoyed to see that you have escaped the jaws of death. Ghatotkacha passed for a worthy reason. He neither lived nor died like a normal rakshasa. He died like a kshatriya guarding dharma from *adharmic* forces. His dying was not futile. Rejoice, do not lament his death."

Krishna's description intrigued Satyaki. He had a niggling doubt, and he had to ask. "If that is what it is, then why did Karna not use Vasavi shakti on Arjuna all these days?" Krishna smiled. "Each night at the Kaurava camp, every discussion between all the war heroes would end with Dushasana, Duryodhana, and Shakuni asking Karna to kill Arjuna with his Vasavi shakti. Karna would agree. He would set out each morning determined to kill Arjuna in a one-on-one encounter, hoping to use Vasavi shakti on him. But I was constantly vigilant. I made sure their chariots did not stay next to each other long enough for a duel to start. I used my yogic powers to make sure his mind was foggy enough for him to forget about his most potent weapon. You will never know all that I have done to guard Arjuna from the Vasavi shakti."

Just then, Vyasadev stepped into the gathering to calm everyone down. "Ghatotkacha's time had come. He was meant to leave today. Remember, he died for the greater good, and you should celebrate, not mourn his sacrifice. Yudhishthir, continue with the war. You will be king on the fifth day from today."

Arjuna started to cry when he heard Krishna. Indeed, the death of Ghatotkacha hurt. Still, the love Krishna had for him was even more heart-rending. *How could someone love another so much?*

Only one thought ruled Krishna's actions: Safeguard those who make the world a better place, where dharma can flourish and *adharma* has no place.

7

THE INFALLIBLE ONE

8.70.28

सूक्ष्मो धर्मो दुर्विदश्चापि पार्थ विशेषतोऽज्ञैः प्रोच्यमानं निबोध ।
प्राप्नुयास्त्वं वधाद्भ्रातुर्नरकं चातिघोरम् ॥

Sookshmo dharmo durvidashchaapi partha visheshtogyaih
prochyamaanam nibodha
Praapnuyaastvam vadhaaddhaaturnarakam chaatighoram

"O Partha! Dharma is subtle and not easily understood,
especially by those lacking wisdom.
Listen carefully: choosing to end your own life instead of
facing your duty will lead to even greater suffering."

Digging deep is key to deciding right from wrong. Beneath every right and every wrong lies a hidden motive. Uncover that motive to know right from wrong.

Vows Too Deep... Or Not?

"You know I will never raise my weapon against you—a woman by birth, and now you have changed into a man. Yet, I have vowed never to kill a woman." Bhishma told Shikhandi who had just released three arrows into his chest.

A generation ago, Bhishma had abducted Amba to marry his brother Vichitravirya, but she was in love with Salva. However, when Bhishma let her go, Salva rejected her. She then turned to Bhishma, who rejected her, too, because of his vow of celibacy. Spurned and enraged that Bishma had ruined her life, Amba had cursed him, "I will kill you in my next birth." Many penances later, Lord Shiva granted her wish to be born to Drupada, Draupadi's brother. Born Shikhandini, she was raised a boy and married off to the princess of Darshana, only to realize later that she was born a woman. Upset by the turn of events, Shikhandini took refuge in a forest, where she exchanged sexes with a yaksha and became Shikhandi, a man.

Despite the blows to his chest, Bhishma continued with the rampage, killing thousands, until Arjuna yet again commanded Shikhandi to pummel him with arrows and kill him. He knew Bhishma would not counter Shikhandi's attacks—his vow would come in the way, as always. Keeping Shikhandi in front of him, Arjuna rained thousands of arrows on Bhishma, piercing every inch of his body until the grand warrior gave up. There were so many arrows piercing his skin that when he fell off his chariot, he did not fall to the ground but lay on a bed of arrows instead. Bhishma had a boon to live for as long as he wanted. So, despite lying on a bed of arrows, defeated, Bhishma, the one with the dreadful vows, chose the time to leave.

It had all started with Bhishma's vow to marry off his father, King Shantanu, to Satyavati, the daughter of the fishing community chief. But Satyavati's father had one condition. "My one and only desire is for Satyavati's son to succeed to the throne. Only if I am assured of this will I approve the marriage." Even though it broke his heart, Shantanu quickly abandoned the wedding plan because he had already designated his son Bhishma as his successor. When Bhishma saw how downcast his father was, he made it his mission to bring joy back into his life. *To fulfill responsibilities toward subjects, a king needs to be happy first.* For the greater good of the kingdom, Bhishma made the ultimate sacrifice. "I vow to remain celibate for the rest of my life. I vow eternal loyalty to the King of Hastinapur and to never marry."

Shantanu passed away, leaving behind two other sons—Chitrangada and Vichitravirya. Chitrangada died fighting a Gandharva in battle, and Vichitravirya died young. The throne became vacant, but Bhishma's vow prevented him from becoming king. Vichitravirya's two wives had two children with the help of Vyasa—Dhritarashtra, who was blind, and Pandu, who died young. Yet again the throne became vacant, and Bhishma's vow forbade him from becoming king.

With time, however, the animosity between the sons of Pandu and Dhritarashtra intensified. Dhritarashtra was forced to ascend the throne despite his physical and mental blindness. A dummy king, Dhritarashtra was completely vulnerable to manipulation by his brother-in-law, Shakuni, and son, Duryodhana, who had swallowed their morals and sense of justice and used the king to run the kingdom according to their whims. This led to the fatherless sons of Pandu being subjected to repeated wrongdoings and multiple instances of extreme danger to their lives. Bhishma could only watch silently because he had sworn eternal loyalty to the throne. He could not speak up, because Dhritarashtra was king. Krishna reminded Bhishma, "Your rigid view about the application of dharma keeps coming in the way of your decisions. You are so dogged about the vow itself that its purpose—the larger good of the kingdom and its people—has slipped your mind entirely. Dharma should not be frozen; rather, it should flow freely. Flexibility is key to preserving dharma. You would not have been so rigid in your commitment had you been more malleable. Countless lives and individuals will suffer because of this singular promise of yours. You could have avoided so much suffering had you broken your vow for the greater good, or readjusted your vow of allegiance to the throne to loyalty to a person worthy of the throne instead. The people of Hastinapur would have been blessed with a wonderful ruler.

Krishna, too, had made a vow, swearing not to touch a weapon during the war. Yet he did readjust his vow. Once, Bhishma was on a rampage against the Pandava forces and was about to use his powerful arrows to kill Arjuna. Seeing his friend in danger, Krishna leaped off the chariot. He picked up a disengaged chariot wheel from the ground and rushed toward Bhishma. Suddenly, that wheel transformed into the dazzling Sudarshana *chakra*, spinning on the tip of his index fingers. Bhishma let go of his bow and prepared to welcome death as he saw the wheel's intensity and Krishna charging toward him. He would have perished had Arjuna not grabbed Krishna by his feet. Even though Arjuna had a grip on his feet, Krishna's wrath was so great that he dragged him a few yards. Krishna had his priorities in order. His vow did not matter in that split second. All that mattered to him was saving selfless people whose existence made a difference to the world.

True Lies

By the fifteenth day of the war, Dronacharya had completely overwhelmed the Pandava army. He was attacking them with divine missiles, killing over twenty thousand men at once. Terror gripped the soldiers. *This person cannot be our acharya! Demons have possessed him!*

On realizing the seriousness of the situation, Krishna said, "We must find a way to convince the acharya to lay down his weapons. Otherwise, the entire army will perish in an instant. That can happen only if Dronacharya believes his son Ashwatthama is dead. He is in this only at his son's behest." Having understood the mission quickly, Bhima rushed off to slaughter Ashwatthama, the elephant.

"Ashwatthama is dead!" Bhima roared with joy. He continued to shout out this news multiple times. Dronacharya, engrossed in a fierce battle nearby, could not believe the words that floated into his ears. He continued fighting. *Ah! I have failed to capture the acharya's undivided attention.* Bhima knew that if there was anyone Dronacharya would believe, it would be Yudhishthir. Bhima had planted a seed of doubt in Dronacharya's mind, enough for him to ask the disciple he trusted most. *Yudhishthir would never lie to me, I know it.* "Yudhishthir, tell me is Ashwatthama dead?"

Krishna had already anticipated this moment. "Yudhishthir, remember, in this particular circumstance, uttering a lie is more important than sticking to the truth. You can save thousands of lives with this single untruth."

Choose a lie that averts the death of thousands over a truth that causes thousands to perish.

Yudhishthir could not lie, but then reluctance to lie changed into a readiness to tell a half-truth once he learned of the elephant Ashwatthama's death. This was the moment of truth for Yudhishthir. So, looking at his acharya, who was waiting for his trustworthy disciple's answer, Yudhishthir replied, "Ashwatthama is dead ... *the elephant.*" Dronacharya could only hear of Ashwatthama's death. His grief did not let him hear the rest. Dronacharya dropped his weapons and sat down on the chariot, surrendering to destiny.

All's Fair

"This is not right, Arjuna! What you are about to do is wrong!"

Karna tried to reason with Arjuna, who had drawn his arrow to shoot at him. He was now an unarmed warrior, his chariot wheel stuck in the ground. "Arjuna, you are on a chariot; I am on the ground. You have weapons; I am weaponless. My misfortune has brought me here. Surely, you are just enough to play fair. You are a hero. You are also righteous. Allow me a moment to release this wheel before we engage in a fair battle again."

Karna was stunned to silence by Krishna's fervent laughter. "Fairness? What fairness are you referring to, Karna? Can you even talk about fairness? Were you fair when you and your friend Duryodhana wickedly conspired against the Pandavas in that assembly hall? Were you fair when you told Dushasana to drag a naked Draupadi to the assembly and call her a prostitute? Were you fair when a sixteen-year-old boy pleaded with you all for a fight? He was weaponless, so he wanted a fair fight, one at a time. Yet all six of you so-called *maharathis* pounced on him together like a pack of ravenous hyenas. Worst of all, when he finally had his weapon, did *you* not cut his bowstring on the sly? Fairness, is it? And now here you are, asking for a fair fight. How can you expect fairness when you have never shown any yourself?"

Karna remained silent—his head hung in shame. Yet despite Krishna's taunts, Karna lifted his bow and released an arrow so powerful that it hit Arjuna in the chest, throwing him off balance to the chariot floor. While Arjuna struggled to return to his feet, Karna returned to trying to release the stuck chariot wheel from the ground. But the wheel remained stuck no matter how much he tried. Krishna shouted to Arjuna, "Behead him before he gets on his chariot." Arjuna quickly cut the flag from Karna's chariot to announce the fall of the great hero. He then pulled out the Anjalika *astra* from his quiver. As he knocked the arrow to his Gandiva bow, the earth trembled. The moment Arjuna released the *astra*, it boomed through the sky and beheaded Karna. The mightiest of warriors had fallen.

Heads I Win, Tails You Lose

Once in Hastinapur, when on a mission to bring peace, Krishna had stayed at Vidura's house. The Kauravas welcomed him, and Duryodhana and Karna escorted him to the courtroom. A lavish celebration was planned to impress Krishna, who would play a pivotal role in determining the outcome of the impending war. Great sages like Narada were invited to the meeting. Duryodhana ensured a lavishly decorated throne for Krishna, hoping to make him feel happy and honored. Duryodhana assumed everything, including loyalty, could be bought.

Duryodhana was quite taken aback when Krishna started speaking freely. Krishna began relating every horrible action the Kauravas had perpetrated against the Pandavas since when they were younger. "Each of your actions was wile enough for the harshest of sentences." Krishna even reprimanded the family elders for their lack of responsibility in punishing the wicked. He then summarized the entire monologue.

"You will find three kinds of people in this world—the true altruists, or those naturally good and live by God's moral principles and fairness; the self-centered, or those who seek benefits; and the repulsive immorals, or those who are unfair and enjoy breaking moral principles. I would not say you belong to the third group, Duryodhana. I refuse to believe that you take pleasure in deceit. My guess is that you prioritize profit over everything else. If that is so, then making the Pandavas your allies would be the most profitable move. Rather than leaning on Karna, Dushasana, and Shakuni, the wiser course of action would be for you to enlist the help of Arjuna and Bhima. With them by your side, none would challenge Hastinapura. Once you befriend them, they will never again try to usurp what you have. Set aside your animosity against the Pandavas if you understand the value of peace. Shed your old useless habits, as a serpent sheds its skin. With this one decision, you can save millions of lives and be the ruler of an unbeatable kingdom."

The significance of your motivations outweighs that of your actions.

Duryodhana refuted all charges Krishna leveled against him. "You just held me responsible for everything that has happened to the Pandavas. Father probably bequeathed the kingdom to the Pandavas out of fear or ignorance. I was too young then, but now that the kingdom is mine, I will not return it. I refuse to part with anything at all.

Duryodhana's response enraged Krishna. "You have conveniently forgotten all your transgressions. You did not even publicly acknowledge Draupadi's humiliation. You did not even mention the plot to burn the Pandavas in Vanavrata. You have no recollection of trying to poison Bhima when you were a child. You are the most wicked person alive. In his frustration, Krishna turned to the family's elders. "Look at what you have created! You failed to discipline him at the right time and encouraged his wild behavior."

Duryodhana's blood boiled because of Krishna's public confession of his mistakes. He wanted him arrested immediately. The Kurus clearly could not bind Krishna because of his immense strength. It was then that Krishna was convinced Duryodhana belonged to the third category of people.

All Is Not Fair

It was the final showdown. Duryodhana was attacking Bhima mercilessly with his mace. Watching the two go at each other, Arjuna asked Krishna, "Who do you think will win? In whose corner is righteousness?"

"They are both students of Balarama. Both have received the same instructions. Bhima is more powerful than Duryodhana but less skilled than him. In a fair fight, Bhima may lose. Bhima had vowed to smash Duryodhana's thighs when he was abusing Draupadi. That is the only way he can kill Duryodhana in this fight." Krishna then looked at Bhima and slapped his thighs.

Bhima was staring at defeat. The moment he saw Krishna, he defied all rules of mace combat and struck Duryodhana's thighs open by hitting him below the waist. Duryodhana coiled down like a squished serpent. Bhima ran to him and shouted, "You made fun of Draupadi. Now repent for your sins." Fury still burning within him, Bhima kicked Duryodhana's head and was about to crush it, when his brother Yudhishthir stopped him. "Stop Bhima. Afterall, he is a king. Respect him. Everyone dear to him has died in this battle. Leave him alone."

Yudhishthir then spoke to Duryodhana with utmost compassion. "Do not lament. Your actions have led you to this consequence. You must now meet death as all your friends, brothers, and followers have. It is time to let go."

Duryodhana did not find any solace in Yudhishthir's words. He did not want his pity as he lay gasping.

Krishna walked up to Yudhishthir. "You have done well, O King. The war is now over." "Yes, the war is over," Yudhishthir acknowledged. The Pandavas burst into celebrations, applauding Bhima for kicking Duryodhana's head. They mocked Duryodhana as they rejoiced.

Krishna, who had not approved of Bhima's last action, spoke. "It is not right to abuse an enemy who has fallen. The wicked Duryodhana has paid for his sins. He is neither foe nor friend now. Ignore him for he is just a lifeless object."

The moment the almost-dead Duryodhana heard Krishna's righteous speech, he was writhing in pain but still questioning everything that happened in this war. "Are you not ashamed, Krishna, to deliver such a hollow speech? Have you forgotten how Bhima defeated me? Had you not used your trickery every step of the way in this war to help the Pandavas, so many of those heroes—Bhishma, Dronacharya, Karna—would not have died. The Pandavas would never have won. Unlike you, I have been fair in war."

Krishna replied, "You and your brothers and friends faced death because of your sinful actions and deeds. I had extended peace and asked you to atone for your sins by giving the Pandava brothers their share of the kingdom. But you refused. For what you did to Draupadi, to Abhimanyu, for your disrespect toward elders, you are on the ground, suffering."

"What does it matter what you say, Krishna? I fought fair, and now I am dying."

Krishna spoke to the Pandavas, "Being good and righteous is not enough. One needs to be practical too. Their vileness would have trampled your righteousness. This is the only way they could have been defeated. The war would have been completely fair had they not broken the moral code first. For good to prevail in this world and for you to win, I had to use my powers. It is only fair to use such means when the enemy is beyond deceitful. You won because you were righteous; they lost because they were not. Now for your own good, lay down your bow and live in peace."

Morality Binds, Wisdom Frees

Morality and ethics are frequently mistaken for one another. Without understanding their actual significance, most people use them interchangeably. To please the Supreme Lord, one must act morally. Humans did not create morality; God created it. Humans made ethics. This is why different cultures, contexts, mindsets, and agendas have different ethical standards. Morality, however, is universal. People often use ethics and morality interchangeably. However, morals take precedence over ethics. Breaking the rules of war is an ethical violation, but lacking compassion for another human violates moral principles. Karna was busy violating every moral principle imaginable when adhering to ethics. Krishna was more focused on adhering to moral principles, so he did not hesitate to violate human ethics for the larger good or if it meant teaching a lesson.

Krishna's discourse with Duryodhana in the Hastinapura courtroom on the three types of people provides insight into his perspective on morality. The altruists act in accordance with more elevated moral standards. By strictly adhering to the right path, they spare no effort to gain God's approval. Their decision-making and way of life are deeply rooted in the *why*. All their actions align with this *why*. They never do what is wrong in God's eyes or violate any moral codes.

The self-centered people view the world through a very egocentric lens. They pounce on a good opportunity when they see it. Their motivation stems from within. Their hearts are like voracious vortices that consume everything surrounding them. They will break any moral code as long as it is of benefit. Although they will ride the moral high horse if that brings them more gain. They could not care less about right or wrong. All they care about is the self.

The immorals are the worst kind. They take pleasure in wrongdoing and find great joy in breaking the rules set by God and the society. They see every act of rebellion as a way to prove their superiority. They seek the thrill that comes from defying authority. They are proud to go against the tide of society.

The altruists need honor and appreciation because they are beacons of society. The self-centered need motivation and education to think on a higher level. The immorals ought to be censured and penalized according to the degree of their transgressions. Perpetrators learn their lessons the hard way. Only when punished for their wrongdoings do they think twice the next time.

Dharma Is Not Rigid

Bhishma had talent and experience, yet his life view was very myopic and self-centered—being loyal to those without merit because of his skewed perception of loyalty and dharmic vows. Krishna was selfless. Because of his profound maturity and wisdom, he could see dharma for its adaptability and practical application in this world.

Krishna's actions were driven by motive, whereas Bhishma's were driven by the action itself. Krishna focused on being practical and committed to the greater good, Bhishma was married to his vows. Krishna prioritized his relationships and his responsibilities; Bhishma was fixated on his public persona as a vow-keeper. Krishna was instrumental in establishing a new tradition of dharmic leadership and selfless governance; Bhishma's rigid commitment to his vows led to the downfall of an entire dynasty. Bhishma is lauded for his unwavering commitment to his vows; Krishna is vilified for bending the rules. Yet the outcomes are clear. After decades of ruling according to dharmic principles, the Pandavas' descendants continued the practice for centuries. For thousands of years, Krishna's teachings have served as an inspiration to many more. When Bhishma died, his legacy died with him.

The Three *Neetis*

Three life ideologies, or *neetis*, help understand ethics and morality better.

1. *Brihaspati Neeti* encourages chastity in all aspects of life. This serves as a powerful reminder to always act in accordance with moral codes and never compromise the principles of dharma. Throughout their lives, the Pandavas followed *Brihaspati Neeti*, never once breaking dharmic codes to exact revenge for wrongs done to them. They never once strayed from the rules of dharma—not when they were on the verge of being burned alive in a lac palace, not when losing all their wealth to gambling, nor when being witness to their wife's public humiliation.

They exercised self-control and stayed within the parameters of Brihaspati dharma.

2. *Kanika Neeti* promotes putting oneself first at all times. One can do whatever one wants to acquire what one wants. The principles of dharma are irrelevant here. Rights and wrongs do not matter. The end justifies the means: If I have my way, it is right. If I fail, it is wrong. Shakuni introduced this ideology to Duryodhana, and he found it very appealing. So, throughout his life, Duryodhana was indifferent to his actions as long as they brought him the results he desired. Morality lectures were useful only if they got him closer to his objective. He would resort to any means necessary to achieve his goal, including discussing ethics. In his pursuit of dominance, which he craved so much, he felt no remorse for any action, be it deceit, insult, conspiracy, manipulation, or even the murder of a child.

3. *Shukra Neeti* is a pragmatic outlook fostered by the idea that to be good, one must be practical. People who lack practical wisdom are easy prey for those with evil intentions. As bad things become worse, good things are buried. Shukracharya gave importance to practicality, preaching that one should not be overconsumed by the desire to do good; rather, one could resort to deceit in a life-or-death situation. Doing so would not make one immoral, instead, it would make one practical. However, one should not assume that everyday is an emergency. Then it no longer remains an emergency. Krishna introduced *Shukra Neeti* to the Pandavas, who were loyal

> proponents of *Brihaspati Neeti*. Not once had Yudhishthir strayed from the tenets of dharma. However, *Brihaspati Neeti* could never stand a chance against *Kanika Neeti*, which is also why the Kauravas always got away with their wrongs. They were certain the Pandavas would never retaliate or ever abandon dharma—not even in a fit of vengeance. Yet, this balance shifted the moment Krishna became a part of the Pandavas' lives. Krishna was certain good people should not suffer for being good, yet he felt it was not right to let bad people enjoy life. Good people should not suffer for the enjoyment of bad people.

The result of Krishna's guidance became evident—the Kauravas, who had a history of abuse and crime, finally started to lose ground to the more tolerant and innocent Pandavas. Krishna introduced *Shukra Neeti* only after the Kauravas broke the first rule of war.

Hard Decisions

An emergency—that is what it was. Yudhishthir had to make the most critical decision of his life—choosing to lie after an entire lifetime of only speaking the truth.

Dronacharya, too, had to make a difficult choice earlier in the war—break the first rule of combat and sneak up on an enemy from behind after an entire lifetime of religiously following and teaching the codes of warfare. Both Yudhishthir and Dronacharya had to make difficult first-time choices.

Dronacharya had no clue Abhimanyu would cause so much chaos by entering the *chakravyuha* he had created. The young boy was absolutely perfect in combat. Not even six *maharathi*s with their full armies could halt him. Dronacharya had to make a quick judgment call as he watched his plan fail and foresaw the impending doom. He told Karna, "Unless someone sneaks up on the boy and destroys his indestructible armor from behind, there is no stopping him." For the first time in his life, Drona uttered something absolutely *adharmic* and extremely shameful for a warrior. Yet, he knew this was the only way.

Yudhishthir's situation was identical. It seemed like Dronacharya would defeat the Pandava army. There was no stopping him for as long as he was armed. Krishna brought up the concepts of *Shukra Neeti* with Yudhishthir. In his opinion, it is not sinful to tell a falsehood if it means saving the lives of thousands of people. Yudhishthir half-lied about Ashwatthama's death with considerable reluctance.

It is necessary to measure the effect of any action. It is truly sinful to lie to further one's nefarious goals at the expense of others. Still, a truth that hurts many people is just as much a sin. So, it is more important to consider the effect of one's words than to just say them.

After the war ended, however, Yudhishthir returned to practicing *Brihaspati Neeti*. Krishna let him be and did not interfere with how he ruled. An emergency was treated as one and never allowed to become the norm.

8

THE INFINITE LORD

5.124.35

पृथक्च विनिविष्टानां धर्मं धीरोऽनुरुध्यते।
मध्यमोऽर्थं कलिं बालः काममेवानुरुध्यते ।।

Prithakcha vinivishtaanaam dharmam dheeronurudhyate
Madhyamoartham kalim baalah kaammevaanurudhyate

When isolated, the wise follow dharma,
the mediocre pursue wealth, which causes strife,
the foolish indulge in lust.

You are what you believe in. You become that which you believe you can become.

Peacelovers, Peacewreckers, and the Peacemaker

"You are the center of our universe!" Yudhishthir lauded Krishna in the assembly in the presence of his closest associates. "You are the one we can always count on, especially when things get rough. Please visit Hastinapura as our envoy and speak with our uncle and his stubborn son. The king appears to have no moral compass. Instead of being a responsible father figure, he is behaving like a desperate thief all because of his obsessive attachment to his son. I do not want a war. Unfortunately, I was born a kshatriya, and I must devote my life to helping others. Had I been born a brahman, I would have begged; had I been born a vaishya, I would have leaned on my business acumen for survival; had I been born a shudra, I would have slaved for someone. But the life of a kshatriya revolves around giving, and for that I need enough money and resources. Much as I hate to send you—our most precious treasure—as our representative to that vile bunch, I am now left with no choice but to request you to go there as our peace emissary. All I can do is warn you that they will do everything in their power to hurt you once you are there."

Krishna's all-knowing smile lit up the room. *Yudhishthir was so naïve! Only this man deserves to rule the world—such humility, such simplicity, a selfless heart that wants nothing more than to serve.* "The Hastinapur court is a haven for sin. So do not expect my peace mission to succeed. I am under no illusion that the Kauravas' innately wicked nature will magically transform after my visit. But I do intend to reveal Duryodhana's genuine character to the world while I am there, officially uncovering the truth to the world that your intentions are good and his are evil. I will go there as your peace negotiator and do what is best for you. But while I am away, get ready for war, because Duryodhana will not change his mind."

Bhima chipped in, surprising everyone. "Yudhishthir's peace proposal is excellent. Krishna, make sure to pacify Duryodhana rather than instigate him with your taunts." Krishna burst out laughing. Sensing Krishna's sarcasm, Bhima became defensive. "Having said that, let me be clear that I am not afraid of war. It is just that I do not support the mindless slaughter of innocent people for someone's ego boost. Siding with Krishna, Arjuna said, "I agree Duryodhana is stubborn. But, Krishna, please make sure you speak to him in a way that preserves Yudhishthir's dignity. I have full faith in your plan, and I know that you will always do what is best for everyone." *O Arjuna! My forever supporter!* The little doubts and debates made Krishna smile. "I am not going there to perform a miracle, rather to make sure that the world does not hold the virtuous Yudhishthir responsible for what is about to happen."

Nothing, however, seemed amusing to someone else in Yudhishthir's courtroom. Draupadi was seething in fury as her husbands went on and on about peace and tolerance. Clutching her disheveled hair, she turned to Krishna, sobbing in rage, "Krishna, do not forget, I have vowed never to tie my hair until I wash it with the blood of Dushasana. Do not forget they publicly humiliated me." Krishna looked at his sister with compassion and kindness. "Trust me, you will be avenged. Duryodhana and his associates will never change, and they will face destruction at the hands of your husbands."

On a *dwadashi*[21] in Kartik[22] during the Maitra *muhurta*[23] when the planets aligned in Revathi *nakshatra*,[24] Krishna left from the Pandavas' abode in Upalavya in the Virata kingdom for Hastinapur. He reached Hastinapur on the third day and entered the city during the Bharani *nakshatra*.[25]

Things looked drastically different in Hastinapura. News of Krishna's arrival as the Pandavas' messenger of peace received mixed reactions. Vidura and Bhishma were so happy to know that their beloved Krishna was paying a personal visit to their city that they began making elaborate arrangements to welcome him. But Dhritarashtra began contemplating ways to buy Krishna's loyalty with gifts. "Your plan is so foolish, Father," Duryodhana said, shooting down his proposal, but going on to suggest an even more preposterous one. "Let us imprison Krishna." His audacity stumped Bhishma and Vidura.

Despite his nefarious intentions, Duryodhana feigned innocence when interacting with Krishna in public. Walking up to him, he said, "I am very hurt that you have rejected our offer of hospitality and instead opted to stay with Vidura. Why have you refused these elaborate and stately arrangements that we made for you?

Such hypocrisy! Krishna, already tipped off by Vidura, knew of Duryodhana's evil plans. He chose to overlook Duryodhana's

---

21 Twelfth day of the lunar calendar.

22 Eighth month.

23 7.36–8.24 am.

24 The twenty-seventh and final nakshatra (or a group of stars). In the **Pisces** constellation, Revati signifies the end of one cycle and the beginning of the next.

25 The second *nakshatra*. In the Aries constellation, *Bharani* signifies letting go of attachments and going with the flow of life.

sense of entitlement and his expectation that he would accept the fake hospitality. Choosing not to stoop to the vile king's level, Krishna replied calmly and truthfully. "I have no interest in your lavish feast. I do not dine at the home of the unrighteous. You are an eternal slave to hatred. The Pandavas are my everything, and you despise them for no apparent reason. I take your hatred toward them very personally. I believe you will lace the food you serve me with animosity and hate. I only have food served by someone who loves me. You have no love for me, so why should I dine at your house?"

Krishna left without waiting for Duryodhana's response, leaving him dumbstruck. Vidura was so happy Krishna had decided to dine at his house. *It is a sign of Krishna's love for me. I am overjoyed, but ....* "Krishna, I worry for your safety here in Hastinapura. I sense danger in every nook. I fear Duryodhana and his supporters will attempt to publicly discredit and insult you." Krishna smiled, "A person headed toward calamity cannot think straight. Duryodhana and his father are on the verge of impending doom. Their insane actions are accelerating the process to their ruin. Someone will have done a great service to humanity if they can put brakes on this reckless duo's race to disaster. But I know well that nothing I do or say will be enough to stop the war. What is important is I let the world know who was set on starting the war and who did everything to stop it. By the end of this peace mission, history will have a clearer image of Yudhishthir's magnanimity and Duryodhana's vindictiveness.

The following morning, Krishna's arresting presence was the center of attention in the courtroom. He emerged like the warm golden rays of the sun rising from behind a dark mountain, in exquisite yellow silken clothes and his favorite necklace with the lustrous *Kaustubha mani*.[26] None seemed to have enough of Krishna's beauty. They sat entranced by his brilliance.

Krishna's thunderous voice jolted them out of their trance. He spoke directly to Dhritarashtra, the king of Indraprastha. "The Pandavas have sent me here as a peacemaker. This house of the Kuru's is on the verge of destruction. The stubbornness of one man has brought the entire human race to this state. The debasement of the once-noblest house in the world is deeply disheartening. The Pandavas have shown patience and restraint by staying out of Hastinapura's affairs, even though they had every right to. Instead, they focused on building their own empire from the ground up. O King, your son is walking the path of sin. He shows a complete lack of empathy and cares only about furthering his own interests; he is rude and ignores sound advice. Because of this dangerous mindset, this world is about to end. The Pandavas are good people. Despite all the wrong done to them their whole lives, they continue to choose the path of righteousness. Yudhishthir chooses not to remember any wrong done to him. A decent person such as him deserves support, respect, and to be given what is rightfully his. Yudhishthir only wants five villages returned—the five that are rightfully his—Avisthala, Vrikasthala, Makandi, Varanavata, and Avasana. He is not demanding that you return his entire kingdom. As a kshatriya, it is his duty to establish a kingdom. His ask is small. O King, if you and your sons are the forest, the

---

26 The most brilliant of the fourteen gems that emerged from the ocean when the gods (devas) and demons (asuras) performed the *Samudra manthana* (ocean churning).

Pandavas are lions that protect the forest. If you kill the lions, you leave the forest vulnerable to indiscriminate tree-felling by woodcutters. In the absence of a forest, where will the lions live? The Pandavas and the Kauravas need each other just as much as the lions and the forest are interdependent. Accept their offer of peace, so that the entire Kuru clan live in peace and harmony."

Everyone nodded in agreement, but Dhritarashtra showed no signs of taking action. Instead, he complained of helplessness. Skirting responsibility, he said, "My son disobeys me. Krishna, you counsel him." Krishna turned to Duryodhana and tried to inspire him with words of wisdom to appeal to his softer side. Bhishma and Vidura tried counseling the prince as well. "Why is everyone pointing their fingers at me? Why should I be the one to listen to your lectures?" Duryodhana said, having completely lost the little patience he had. "Tell me, who rolled the dice? Did I coerce him? He was miserable at it, and he lost—fair and square. How is his loss my fault? He made those awful choices during the dice game, and now you are here taking their side and pinning the blame on me! That is something! We have done nothing to harm them, yet they are trying to pick a quarrel. I am a kshatriya, too. If challenged, I will not back down from a fight. I would rather break than bend as any good kshatriya. I was a minor at the time of the kingdom's division. I had no say in it. It is father's mess, not mine. Hereon, I cannot allow such mistakes to be repeated. For as long as I am alive, I will not give the Pandavas any land—not even the size of a pinhead.

Roaring laughter filled the courtroom, terrorizing everyone. Krishna stood up, his intense gaze revealing his wrath. "It seems as if you are dying to meet your end, Duryodhana. You will soon witness the dance of death on the battlefield. How dare you claim innocence? You have no right to pretend that you are not guilty. You act innocent despite having insulted Draupadi in front of an entire assembly. Radheya, your friend, and Dushasana, your brother, verbally abused her and called her names no woman should ever have to hear. You claim innocence despite having tried to poison Bhima when he was a child and attempting to kill the Pandavas and their mother. After many failed attempts at harming the Pandavas, you have the audacity to wash your hands off all your horrific crimes in front all these witnesses."

Duryodhana leaped off his seat and left the courtroom in a huff, even as Krishna was speaking. All the elders in the courtroom were startled by his disrespectful attitude. An embarrassed Dhritarashtra enlisted his wife, Gandhari's help to reason with her son. After much cajoling, Duryodhana returned to the courtroom, but with an even nastier attitude. Having realized that Krishna had completely cornered him in front of everyone, Duryodhana shouted, "Arrest Krishna and enchain him." Jaws dropped in the assembly hall as people became aware of his sinister intentions. Soldiers marched in with chains, in blind obeyance of their king's orders.

Supreme Revelation

Just then, before anyone could react, everyone was blinded by a sudden burst of light. The only ones who could see what was happening were the great sages gathered in the hall, Bhishma, Dronacharya, Vidura, and Duryodhana. The intense light was emanating from Krishna's body. He rose from his seat and, with his head pressed against the lofty ceiling of the royal courtroom, started to swell tremendously. Krishna had grown enormous in no time.

Then suddenly, hundreds of divine entities appeared on different parts of Krishna's body—on his forehead was Lord Brahma, the co-creator of the universe; on his wide chest, the eleven Rudras; and on his shoulders sat Indra, Varuna, and Yama, the gods of the heavens, seas, and death, as well as Kubera, the guardian of the gods' wealth. His mouth spouted Agni, the god of fire. Krishna seemed to have absorbed all of the universe's deities in that enormous form that he had taken on. He even had the five Pandavas in his gigantic right hand. Many arms, holding massive, lethal weapons, sprang out of his torso. Those fortunate to witness this overwhelming and otherworldly vision bowed in awe—everyone except Duryodhana. He spoke with disdain, "Krishna, are you trying to pull off magic to deceive everyone into giving in to your demands?"

As Duryodhana continued to argue with Krishna, Dhritarashtra shouted, "I have seen it! Oh, I have seen it all!" *Did he say "see"? Can he see now?!* It took everyone a moment before they realized that Dhritarashtra could actually see Krishna's divine manifestation. The ever-deprived-of-sight king could see for the first time in his life. "Krishna, now that I have seen you, there is nothing else I want to see. You can take my vision away now," Dhritarashtra said, tears streaming down his face.

Krishna then reverted to his original two-armed form and left the courtroom. The euphoria in the court faded the moment Krishna walked out. As Krishna was preparing to mount his chariot, Dhritarashtra rushed out and made a final plea. "Krishna! My son is completely out of my hands. You have seen that for yourself. Your journey to mediate a truce between your warring cousins has been futile. But know this, I do not hate the Pandavas. Please do not harbor any animosity toward me. I tried my best, what more can I do?"

With one foot on the chariot's footboard, Krishna turned around to deliver his final verdict. "Listen, all you wise men and women of Hastinapur. All of you were witness to my efforts to prevent war, to Duryodhana's stubbornness, and to Dhritarashtra's declaration of helplessness. The consequences are neither in my control nor yours. What will follow is the consequence of your collective powerlessness and Duryodhana's idiocy."

Saying this Krishna left, his chariot leaving a cloud of dust. As the chariot faded from view, so did all hope. While the residents of Hastinapur struggled through the night, Krishna slept soundly, content that he had done his best.

Just as peeling away the layers of the onion reveals the soft bulb, peeling back the superficial layers of every event in life reveals true knowledge. Most people would focus on the thin, dry outer layer of Krishna's peace mission; however, intelligent people will peel back layer after layer to see the softer unseen center that Krishna revealed through his seemingly unsuccessful peace mission.

Nine Layers

During his peace mission, Krishna peeled away nine invisible layers.

Layer 1: As a messenger of peace, Krishna was essentially balancing the lives of countless innocent people. It was not a fear of conflict that led him to assume the role of peacemaker. He desired peace, but he was ready for war. He volunteered to be a peacemaker because he was aware that a conflict would have a devastating effect on everyone—peace lovers, peace seekers, peace brokers, peacemakers, or peacewreckers. So he worked hard to facilitate a mutually agreeable resolution to the political crisis the society was experiencing at the time.

***Layer 2*:** Krishna disapproved of cowardly peace proclamations. When someone seeks peace for fear of war, it's just a coward seeking refuge in a truce. Dhritarashtra, Bhishma, and Dronacharya exemplified that in Hastinapur. Arjuna, too, advocated for such a truce just before the fight. Such peace seekers suggested allowing the Kauravas to do as they pleased. But Krishna refused to give in to the depravity of the wicked. He was against any peace treaty that gave in to evil or condemned people to a life devoid of honor, dignity, and higher values. His goal was to bring lasting and meaningful peace.

***Layer 3*:** Draupadi epitomized hope for all women. If the perpetrators who publicly shamed a queen were allowed to escape punishment, guaranteeing her neither safety nor justice, imagine the inconceivable misery of the women who neither had the authority nor the voice. As a social reformer, Krishna stood for women's rights. As a peace messenger, one of his duties was to tell the people assembled and future generations that what happened to Draupadi was wrong and that he would put an end to the savage cruelty such wicked men perpetrated.

***Layer 4*:** It was important to expose the real warmongers for posterity and lay the blame where it belonged. Through the public discussion with Duryodhana and Dhritarashtra in Hastinapur, Krishna revealed their true nature to historians to ensure that the blame rested on the Kauravas—the ones responsible for the war.

***Layer 5*:** Some people were fence-sitters. Krishna coerced all of them into taking a side. Under the pretext of emergency, Bhishma, Dronacharya, and Kripa had remained indecisive for far too long. Krishna forced them to make their real allegiance clear. After the peace mission, they had no choice but to join forces with either the Pandavas, who represented the altruistic dharmic mentality, or the Kauravas, who represented the egocentric *adharmic* mindset.

***Layer 6*:** Beyond the opinions of the royal family lay the general public's take on the issue. Up until the peace mission, the public's stance was vague and uncertain. But Krishna successfully swayed public opinion in the Pandavas' favor through his diplomatic peace mission.

Layer 7*:** Krishna always knew that Duryodhana was beyond redemption. However, his primary motivation behind agreeing to negotiate peace was to prevent Duryodhana from dragging innocent people into the conflict to protect himself. People with malicious intent would accuse Krishna of failing to prevent the war when he had the opportunity if he did not try. He was determined to give it his all one last time, believing that if the Kauravas just heard him out, much destruction would be averted. To achieve this, he spoke using ***laghu kritam (words that cannot be taken lightly), ***agrastam*** (words that are precise and unambiguous), ***anirastam*** (words that cannot be challenged), ***asankulam*** (words spoken calmly to appeal to the heart), ***hetumat*** (words backed by logic and reason), and ***uttamam*** (words chosen carefully).

***Layer 8*:** Krishna wanted to build mental pressure. First, he came from Dwaraka to Hastinapur in a chariot laden with the mightiest weapons, signaling his intention to destroy evil. Second, he replaced his regular charioteer Daruka with Satyaki, the second most powerful warrior, implying that they were prepared for a small battle, if necessary. Third, Krishna turned down Duryodhana's carefully planned royal hospitality and chose to stay with Vidura, sending a strong message to the royalty and adding mental pressure on them, because Duryodhana's loss of face was all anyone in Hastinapur could talk about.

***Layer 9*:** Krishna's visit impacted every single person differently, especially after the Vishwaroop darshan. Before the Vishwaroop darshan, the courtroom was in a state of diplomatic and rational discourse, but after it, the realm became divine. The indescribable event could only be experienced, not verbalized. It evoked different reactions, touching everyone differently—remorse planted the seed of change in some people; a new awareness set some on course to atone for their sins; for some, it brought back memories of past mistakes and feelings of dread; it moved some to a greater level of self-awareness and accountability; it severely harmed the self-esteem of others. Regardless of the impact, everyone left that hall a different person.

9

THE COMPASSIONATE LORD

11.26.4

मृतं वा यदि वा नष्टं योऽतीतमनुशोचति ।
दुःखेन लभते दुःखं द्वावनर्थौं प्रपद्यते ॥

Mrtam va yadi va nashtam
yotitamanushochati
Duhkhena labhate duhkham
dvaavanarthom prapadyate

"Dwelling on the past—whether mourning the lost or the departed—only deepens sorrow, bringing suffering twice over."

The soul can never be cut into pieces by any weapon, nor can it be burned by fire, nor moistened by water, nor withered by the wind.

Experience cold or heat, pleasure, or pain.
These experiences are fleeting; they come and go.
Bear them patiently.

Lamentations

Eighteen days were spent in combat. After that, nothing remained but a sea of decomposing corpses. The Pandavas won, but no one was celebrating. The Kauravas lost, but no one was left to feel the pain of defeat. Those who escaped the massacre were traumatized for life.

For the first time in fourteen years, the Pandavas were headed home for Hastinapura. They had barely set out when a shrill cry stopped them. It was as if the entire universe was crying inconsolably, and the world would collapse in sorrow. The wail sounded like the melancholic chorus of a thousand voices.

Krishna and Satyaki led the Pandavas as they made their way back to the battlefield. Following their cousin like sheep, the brothers, heartbroken from the loss of sons and relatives, carried their grief with them. The battlefield was a mess of thousands of women crying uncontrollably over the mangled bodies of their husbands, sons, and kin. Dhritarashtra stood right in the middle, surrounded by his one hundred grieving daughters-in-law. The elderly blind monarch, tied to the spot by the writhing knots of pathos, did not know which way to turn. His sons were precious all the same.

Unable to bear the debilitating pain his uncle was experiencing, Yudhishthir sprinted over to the old king and fell to his feet. Dhritarashtra, unmoved by Yudhishthir's emotional reaction, subconsciously lifted up his nephew and held him in his cold embrace. Dhritarashtra's public composure concealed his inner rage and turmoil. The helpless father's intense wrath grew as he remembered Bhima, the one who killed all his hundred sons. Instead, he held out his arms for Bhima, beckoning him to a loving embrace. Just as Bhima was about to step forward, Krishna put his hand on his shoulder and pulled him back. Bhima sensed Krishna's apprehension and stopped.

Krishna rushed to the Kaurava camp and returned with a large iron sculpture exactly matching Bhima's build. Duryodhana had created it to practice hitting. The sculpture was pounded, twisted, and dented in several places—proof of Duryodhana's wrath and frustration toward the Bhima. Krishna held his breath as he pushed the statue closer to Dhritarashtra, hoping the emotionally unstable blind king would not sense the exchange.

The moment Dhritarashtra held the Bhima replica, his anger exploded. As he felt the rippling muscles, he pulled Bhima's replica closer into his death grip and began squeezing him with all his might. Dhritarashtra was visually challenged but not physically challenged. He possessed the strength of ten thousand elephants, and his lethal embrace crushed the sculpture into a mangled iron mass. He calmed only when there was nothing left.

What have I done? Suddenly, Dhritarashtra's guilt kicked in. He was responsible for the accidental death of his nephew. He began to apologize profusely. "Oh Bhima! What have I done? Please forgive me. You all know I did not mean to kill him. Forgive me, forgive me, forgive me..." Everyone watched Dhritarashtra going through a gamut of emotions within seconds—from sorrow to apathy to fury to cruelty to guilt to shame.

Bhima was horrified. The monarch, whose chest was gushing blood from metal abrasions, had passed out of exhaustion and dropped next to the mangled metal. Sanjaya, the king's assistant, and confidant, rushed to resuscitate the unconscious king. Dhritarashtra woke up with a start. "This was never meant to happen. This cannot have happened. Forgive me, forgive me..."

Krishna waited until Dhritarashtra's violent wrath abated. "Bhima is not dead," he told Dhritarashtra. "You hugged an iron replica to death."

"Please forgive me, forgive me, forgive…!" Krishna finally addressed the old king's continuous implorations for mercy. "You must accept the Pandavas and Bhima with love. They have lost a lot, too. It is time you forgive them for their mistakes, accept their choices, stop dwelling on the past, and the future." Dhritarashtra realized the futility of harboring resentment and chose to forgive Bhima and move on to the next chapter of his life. He opened his arms for Bhima, yet again, now yearning for a tender embrace. Bhima walked closer and surrendered himself to the elder's warm hug—both letting go of all malice.

Blind Fury

As Krishna was tending to Dhritarashtra's emotional wounds and healing him, elsewhere on the battlefield a volcano erupted. A disheveled Gandhari was angry-crying and pointing at the Pandavas, about to hurl a curse at them. Vyasa stepped in, right at that moment. "My dear child, do not release that thought. Your mind is thinking all the wrong things right now. I can sense your anger and your desire to direct it at the Pandavas. I know you want to curse them, but just know this, it is not the right thought process at all. You are caught in this whirl of incredible affection for your sons, but somewhere that heart of yours holds deep resentment against the Pandavas. Have you forgotten your own words? Do you recall the conversation with your son just before the battle, when he had come seeking your blessings? Let me remind you of the wise words that escaped your mouth. All he wanted was for you to say, 'You will be victorious in this war.' He insisted that you say it because he was dying to hear it. But you conveyed a profound message to him instead. 'Victory,' you said, 'is where dharma is.' You refused to tell your son he would win, no matter how much he begged you. It was obvious to you the whole time that he would lose this war. You also knew why—his unjust and unfair cause. Despite all that you have endured, you have been the world's most patient woman. Please do not fall prey to anger and undo all the good that you have accomplished. Abandon the thought right now. The Pandavas do not deserve your anger."

Oblivious to the Pandavas walking in, Gandhari said to Vyasa, "O great one, I am not upset with the Pandavas for winning this war. My sons' deaths briefly pained me, but I eventually came to terms that this war was their doing and that the Pandavas had no choice but to act. But my blood boils … my soul sears … over two questions that have been gnawing at my mind and I cannot find any answers to: Why did Bhima drink his brother's blood? Why did he use unfair means to kill Duryodhana?"

When he heard her, Bhima felt obligated to answer these questions that were bothering her. He walked up to Gandhari and sat down at her feet. Krishna noticed Bhima's change of tone. He was speaking in his baby voice. "My dear mother, I admit that I made an unfair move to kill Duryodhana. I did it because I was left with no other choice. His immense power was beyond my control, and if I did not do what I did, he would have killed me. It was my last resort, an act of self-defense. Duryodhana is the best fighter in the world. On a level playing field, he is unbeatable. Your son is so powerful that not even the king of the heavens can defeat him. But he abused his power and tormented us for the longest time. He led a life of sin. But more importantly, I had vowed to break his thigh when, in the assembly hall, Duryodhana had exposed it and mocked us all by asking Draupadi to sit on it. No one, least of all, you, can fault me for this. You would have justified it, too, had I smashed his thigh that very second. I had to wait this long to fulfill my vow, only because my brother intervened back then."

Gandhari felt pacified, as if Bhima's confession was a balm to her burning heart. "Your praise for my son and declaring him the world's greatest warrior has touched my heart. I forgive you even though what you did was unfair. But it still breaks my heart that you could even consider consuming Dushassana's blood. How will you justify that?

Bhima pleaded guilty—again. "In my state of extreme rage in the assembly hall, where Dushassana had disrobed Draupadi, I had vowed to tear open his cruel heart and drink his blood. The vow was made in a fit of passion, but I was obligated to fulfill it, nonetheless. While on the day of your son's death, it may have seemed like I drank his blood. But believe me, I did not let a drop of blood pass beyond my lips and teeth. Karna was there. Had he been alive, he would have confirmed this." Guilty of his actions and apologetic, Bhima fell at Gandhari's feet, "Mother, I have wronged you, please forgive me."

Gandhari was still in tears. "*You* killed them all. You killed them *all*. You have now left this elderly man without an heir and this old blind couple without anyone to lean on. Could you not spare at least one of my hundred sons?"

Almost ignoring Bhima's pleas, she asked, "Where's that

king of yours?" Yudhishthir rushed forward and fell to her feet. Bhima stood up and retreated a few steps. Yudhishthir said, "Mother, I take full responsibility for the war and the tragedy," before Gandhari could even say a word. "Curse me, Mother. I am responsible for the deaths of all your sons." Yudhishthir's plea reminded her of Vyasa's advice. She regained her composure and chose forgiveness. Her heart had calmed down, but her spirit was still restless. She was about to turn away when, through the gap beneath her blindfold, she spotted Yudhishthir's fingernail as he held her feet. Within moments, his fingernail was charred black. *Oh! what power!* Arjuna quickly ducked behind Krishna as he witnessed the manifestation of Gandhari's wrath. The other brothers stepped aside too.

True Vision

As the brothers took leave and went to meet their mother and wife, Gandhari was still mourning her sons' death. Although she had obscured her vision with the blindfold, through yogic sadhana,[27] she could see the bloody battlefield strewn with lifeless bodies. As she approached her son Duryodhana's lifeless body, she kneeled and caressed his stiff, bloody hair. She spotted Krishna standing motionless next to her. Suddenly, Gandhari's anger swelled up again. She directed it all against Krishna, who appeared to stand unconcerned and unmoved by all the pain around him.

---

[27] deep meditation

"Your callousness is the root of all the suffering in this world right now. You could have averted the war, yet you decided not to. You could have remained impartial, yet you chose the Pandavas. You could have prevented this destruction and restored peace between the feuding cousins if you had wanted to. I curse you using all the power I have gained from years of *tapasya*. Just as you have brought about the demise of the Kuru clan through this fratricidal war, I curse that thirty-six years from today, you will witness the demise of your own family through a fratricidal war. Just as the women of the Kuru are weeping in grief right now, the Vrishni women will weep too. This curse of Gandhari will be fulfilled."

Krishna's face lit up with a smile.

He is smiling … over a curse, not a boon. What an extraordinary response! Taken aback, the Pandavas realized that Krishna was not an ordinary being.

Krishna spoke to Gandhari with affection. "Thank you for cursing me. This curse has solved a big problem of mine. Not even the gods have the power to vanquish the Vrishnis. Only they can bring their own demise. Their purpose has been served. I was seeking a means to end their existence. Your curse was just what I needed. Besides, your anger found the right outlet. That makes me even happier. You can no longer harm the Pandavas now that you have spent your anger. The Pandavas are my life, and I was concerned about the possibility of you cursing them." The five brothers' eyes moistened as they heard Krishna. He had taken on his own family the curse meant for them.

"Dharma should be the center of our lives," Krishna continued to tell Gandhari. "All your sorrow, all that pain in your heart is the result of your son choosing the path of *adharma*.

You blame me for all your losses instead of repenting for your mistakes. Remember that your deep attachment to your son prevented you from showing him the right path every time he took the wrong one. You made an even bigger mistake by letting your brother, Shakuni, influence your decisions and interfere with your household affairs. The chaos surrounding you now is the outcome of your callous disregard for whatever was going on in your home. In Hastinapur, you saw me try to talk your son into a peaceful settlement. You also saw his refusal to cooperate. You knew about the plan to burn down the house of lac, yet you turned the other way. Your son committed every single sin in your presence. Yet, not once did you reprimand him. Your attachment has always clouded your vision. You are a righteous woman, but you chose to be blind to your son's wrongdoings. Now that all is gone, you find it easier to shift the blame onto me when it is yours to take. You rightly told your son that victory would be where dharma is, even when he wanted you to wish him victory. You chose dharma then. But now you are letting your sorrow disregard dharma. Let go of your sorrow and look for peace in the truth."

Those words hurt. Those words healed. Gandhari took a deep breath. She was now ready to move on.

Healing Hearts

Everyone copes with adversity differently. Grounding could help some people slow down their racing thoughts, but it does not work for everyone. Some methods only exacerbate the problem. Anger and other powerful emotions flood our systems after a traumatic event. As a natural reaction to pressure, people feel the need to unleash their anger on other people. After experiencing trauma, some feel confined and powerless. This is especially true for those trying to recover from the trauma caused by their own mistakes. People not only feel stuck but also feel imprisoned in a never-ending cycle of pessimism. The only way to heal from trauma is to find help to challenge negative thoughts. Not all decisions we make are correct. Sometimes, our choices lead us down the wrong path, and these choices serve as the catalyst for many things that hurt us. We can move forward only when we do not blame others—even if they are directly or indirectly involved in our situation—and take complete responsibility for our choices. Only that will set us free.

Dhritarashtra would repress his feelings until he reached the point of violent outbursts. As he experienced heightened emotions, which he let out on Bhima, his coping technique intensified his anguish. Krishna's intervention at the last moment helped dispel his pain. Krishna helped him see that the trauma he was going through was entirely his fault and stemmed from his own choices.

You cannot wish away your past. But by embracing it, you can change your future. Bereavement can result from any type of trauma or obstacle. It is okay to be sad and helpful to cry, but it is not okay to wallow in your sorrow. Trauma brings with uncertainties and questions. But it is important to try and find answers. Yet when people cannot find answers, feelings of loss, embarrassment, fear, failure, and humiliation engulf their minds. This is a pessimistic view of things. When depressed, it is hard to assess what could have led to our current situation because reflecting requires courage. Looking back could reveal our own mistakes that led us to this point. It is important to face our past realities head-on to move forward.

A broken heart needs healing, and Krishna is the healer.

Krishna, the healer

Empathy, expertise, wisdom, and self-improvement are the pillars of healing, and Krishna exemplifies these qualities.

Empathy motivates a healer to tend to wounded spirits. Krishna demonstrated true healing by freely giving to others without regard to his own needs, encouraging everyone to realize their full potential.

A healer's expertise lies in mastering mental health issues and dealing with the intricate human mind. Krishna was aware of Dhritarashtra's plan. Therefore he ensured that Dhritarashtra released his anger on the metal statue and then meet Bhima with a healed mind. Krishna was aware of Gandhari's seething anger. So, he approached Gandhari to keep the Pandavas safe even before she spoke to them.

Wisdom lies in knowing when and how to use one's knowledge to navigate complex and unpredictable situations. Krishna examined each situation from different perspectives to help distressed individuals find their own solutions.

A healer must reach a higher level of self-development to help people struggling with their healing journey. Krishna helped others develop awareness so that they could become emotionally stable and gain insight.

Krishna's healing powers helped guide everyone to peace.

II

THE WISDOM OF *THE BHAGAVAD GITA*

What have you lost that you cry for?
What did you bring with you that you have lost?
What did you create that was destroyed?
What you took, you took from here (me).
What you returned was returned here (to me).
What belongs to you today belonged to someone yesterday, and will be someone else's tomorrow.

From "Until Later" to Steadfastness

Snooze. Scroll. Stream. Repeat. This is Alex's life every single day. A chronic procrastinator, he starts his day by postponing waking up, postponing anything constructive by being a slave to social media and TV. *Will do later.* Alex, paralyzed by laziness, lets hours and days go by as he pushes his responsibilities to another hour, another day. Are you an Alex?

Laziness is reluctance to do anything. Procrastination is a reluctance to do important things and wasting time on unimportant things. Both stem from ignorance. Procrastination is deep, but laziness lies deeper in the impact it causes and the effect it creates in a person. Ignorance is masked sorrow that gives an illusion of joy. Unless you shake off the little pebble in your shoe, you can never feel comfortable. Similarly, your procrastination will always make you uneasy because you know you are wasting your potential. In the *Bhagavad Gita*, Krishna has a solution—*sthairyam* (BG 13.8), meaning steadfastness or determination.

BG 18.39

यदग्रे चानुबन्धे च सुखं मोहनमात्मनः ।
निद्रालस्यप्रमादोत्थं तत्तामसमुदाहृतम् ॥ ३९ ॥

Yadagre chaanubandhe cha sukham mohanamaatmanah
nidraalasyapramaadottham tattaamasamudaahrtam

"That happiness which keeps one unaware of true wisdom, which is deceptive from start to finish, and which arises from laziness, sleep, and illusion—such happiness is considered to be of the lowest nature."

In a nutshell, it means there is no pleasure in laziness; it leads to pain from the beginning to the end. The main reason you procrastinate on any crucial task is your dread of the painful beginning. The main reason you are lazy is that it is effortless. In both cases, you are aware of the pain or discomfort associated with doing something. As a species, humans are hardwired to minimize or completely avoid pain and maximize pleasure. Procrastination and laziness, for example, appear painless and provide an illusion of pleasure, but are, in fact, harmful behaviors and sources of pain.

This verse is spot on as it states that it is delusional to think that laziness brings joy because it brings none. It is nothing but a cake baked with pain from start to finish, inside and out. A lazy person cannot be a happy person. Self-loathing grows a little each day in a procrastinator. The self-hate mounts in tandem with the mountain of piling tasks. A deeper analysis will reveal that at the root of procrastination lies your inability to manage your emotions. Emotional regulation comes from managing some very simple basic habits.

BG 6.16

नात्यश्नतस्तु योगोऽस्ति न चैकान्तमनश्नतः ।
न चातिस्वप्नशीलस्य जाग्रतो नैव चार्जुन ॥ १६ ॥

Naatyashrnatastu yogosti na chaikaantamanashrnatah
Na chaatiswapnashilasya jaagrato naiva chaarjuna

"O Arjuna, one cannot attain the state of a yogi by overeating or by eating too little, by oversleeping or by not getting enough rest."

A yogi maintains a balanced routine—neither eating nor sleeping too much nor too little. Regulation is incredibly powerful. Sleep and food are basic human needs. To most people, these are merely physical needs. But the truth is that they also help regulate your emotional needs. So, start by regulating your sleep and food intake. You can regulate your emotions just by eating and sleeping right. Harmonizing your sleeping and eating habits enhances sattva guna—the energy that encourages activity—and lowers tamas guna—the energy that fuels inactivity.

Although Krishna makes specific mention of the regulation of food and sleep, he also obviously refers to the regulation of all aspects of life, including the time you spend on your phone. Too much of anything is detrimental to the emotional well-being of a person. Monitor and control the time you spend on any one activity. Regulate it as soon as it starts leaning toward the excessive. Only a state of balance helps achieve optimal human body and mind function, not extreme indulgence or severe deprivation. Establishing a routine brings everything into a state of balance. Balancing emotions helps get a much better grip on mood. Getting a better grip on mood helps focus on priorities.

BG 3.8

नियतं कुरु कर्म त्वं कर्म ज्यायो ह्यकर्मणः ।
शरीरयात्रापि च ते न प्रसिद्ध्येदकर्मणः ॥ ८ ॥

Niyatam kuru karma tvam karma jyaayo hyakarmanah
Sharirayaatraapi cha te na prasidhyedakarmanah

"One should carry out one's prescribed duties, as action is better than inaction.
Without engaging in work, even the body cannot be sustained."

Do what you love and what you are a natural at. Working is essential for survival, and happiness can come only from doing something that feels satisfying. Krishna's advice for when you feel reluctant to do something you have to is to dig deeper and ask yourself why you feel unmotivated. You just might find out that you are stuck doing things you dislike. So, it is important you do what you love doing and avoid doing what you hate. If you find yourself procrastinating, it is likely that your mind is revolting against having to do something you find uninteresting. Your energy levels will soar once you start doing what you love. No matter how difficult, you will complete tasks only if it is meaningful to you and aligns with your natural talents and interests. A productive mindset is the fruit of such alignment.

BG 3.20

कर्मणैव हि संसिद्धिमास्थिता जनकादयः ।
लोकसङ्ग्रहमेवापि सम्पश्यन्कर्तुमर्हसि ॥ २० ॥

Karmanaiva hi samsiddhimaasthitaa janakaadayah
Lokasangrahamevaapi sampashyankartumarhasi

"Great kings like Janaka achieved perfection through duty. You too should fulfill your responsibilities to set an example for the welfare of the world."

Janaka and other kings set a benchmark for success by choosing work that aligned with their natural inclination. Seek help when struggling. Asking for help is not a sign of weakness but a sign of intelligence. However, asking the wrong person for help when struggling with procrastination is definitely foolish. Be selective about your sources of inspiration. One struggler cannot help another. Find yourself a Janaka who has overcome procrastination. Observe and learn from these Janakas. Talk to them. Engage with them. Spend time with them. Find out what helps them avoid distractions and sustain their motivation, discipline, and focus.

Krishna's tips for Alex

- Be determined.
- Set and follow a routine.
- Regulate your routine.
- Know that laziness is nothing but constant pain.
- Align tasks and jobs that interest you.
- Ask wise people for help.

From "I am a Loser" to Feeling Hopeful

Suramya was brooding alone in darkness—her belongings and empty pill bottles scattered around a once-bright room. The colors in her life had faded into a monochrome abyss. She found herself sinking into an overwhelming depth of despair—every breath stifled under the weight of hopelessness. She sat contemplating the worst in her darkest moments. Do you feel as hopeless as Suramya? Can she (or you) feel hopeful again?

Being understood is the human heart's greatest need and biggest source of hope. Only when there is hope can a person heal from intense pain. Despair is infinite hopelessness, but a hopeless person who has not lost *all* hope (a hopeful person) can only overcome despair by seeking hope from a hope giver.

Krishna says *asha*—hope—arises when *atma-vinigrahah*—a self-controlled or hopeful person—takes *acharyopaasanam*—the shelter of a sensitive hope-giver (BG 13.8).

Just before the most important war in Arjuna's life, he finds himself suffering from severe despair. In fact, he admits it by saying:

BG 2.7

कार्पण्यदोषोपहतस्वभावः
पृच्छामि त्वां धर्मसम्मूढचेताः ।

Kaarpanyadoshopahatasvabhaavah
prichhaami tvaam dharmasammudhachetaah

"I am now uncertain about my duty and overwhelmed by weakness,
leaving me restless and unsettled."

Overthinking, extreme traumatic suffering, weakness of heart, self-centeredness, and loss of composure could all force the kind of mental exhaustion that could contribute to confusion and lack of clarity about one's duties and responsibilities, which in turn could result in inaction.

Many reasons could trigger despair, but the outcome is always the same—insurmountable pain. The natural inclination in such situations is to withdraw, fold in, and shun human connection. Just as a moth seeks refuge in a flame only to be destroyed by it when in despair, you seek refuge in the dark corner of the mind only to spiral deeper into the abyss of negativity. Soon, you become so emotionally detached and spin so far away from human connections that it becomes almost impossible for you to reach out to anyone, no matter how physically close they may be.

All you need is a single human touch to start the healing process, but it takes courage to ask for help. If you have experienced the pain of being judged, chances are you will avoid reaching out. When in despair, you become vulnerable to insensitive thoughts, words, and actions and clam up like the touch-me-not plant, going deeper into darkness.

But Arjuna mustered courage amid extreme mental exhaustion and reached out to Krishna for help.

BG 2.7 (contd.)

यच्छ्रेयः स्यान्निश्चितं ब्रूहि तन्मे
शिष्यस्तेऽहं शाधि मां त्वां प्रपन्नम् ॥ ७ ॥

yachchhreyah syaannishchitam bruhi tanme
shishyasteaham shaadhi maam tvaam prapannam

"In this state, I seek Your guidance on what is truly best for me.
I surrender to You as Your disciple—please instruct me."

Arjuna surrendered himself completely to Krishna to give him shelter, direction, and hope and handhold him through the ordeal emotionally, mentally, and spiritually.

It is important to avoid disengaging from other human connections and the world if you want to overcome any form of despair. While the root of all pain lies in negative human interactions, all joy and hope springs from positive human interactions. Finding a hope-giver can be a lifesaver. Hope-givers stay by your side, physically and emotionally, when times are tough, and are willing to walk with you through your pain—either silently or with words of comfort. Deep despair can throw you into a never-ending whirlpool of self-pity, driving you to harbor negativity and lose every ounce of self-esteem. This state of zero-ness becomes a pity magnet—the endless showers of pity from everyone around become so oddly "comforting" that you find yourself firmly attached to your despair long enough to never see a ray of hope. A hope-giver will not pity you and push you deeper into despair but will show you that ray of hope you cannot see when drowning in the abyss of pain. A hope-giver will walk you back to normalcy.

Despair can force you to stop all physical activity and become physically and mentally disorganized. Finding structure and routine and engaging in physical activity can activate happy hormones and calm your mind. This can help you take baby steps to organize not just your surroundings but also your mind.

Despair can make you too selfish, so much so that your pain appears to be the most insurmountable. Taking time out for *seva* or noble deeds is a powerful way to overcome pain. Serving others in need can help you become more grateful for your life. Gratitude can help you enjoy and appreciate the little things and have a more positive outlook.

Arjuna put the two words of Krishna *atma-vinigrahah* and *acharyopaasanam* into practice in his life to overcome his despair. He first became *atma-vinigrahah*—a self-controlled or hopeful person. He did not disengage from human connections despite the urge to cut off from humanity and fade away into the forest. Instead, he chose a genuine connection. He chose *acharyopaasanam*—seeking the shelter of a hope-giver. He sought Krishna's guidance on making his way out of his despair and submitted to him. Krishna did not pity Arjuna. Instead, he allowed him to embrace normalcy, helped him regain focus on the job at hand, engage in responsible actions, and showed him that the purpose of his life was not to have more but to serve more.

The Suramyas of this world can follow Arjuna's path to overcome their despair and usher in hope when they feel hopeless.

Krishna's tips for Suramya

- Seek human connections.
- Find and surrender to a hope-giver.
- Engage in positive physical activity.
- Serve others in need.

From Arrogance to Humility

Amelia is an overachiever. She receives accolades, awards, and appreciation for everything she does. Recently, she was awarded for a prized and groundbreaking project. Since then, Amelia's vanity has become unbearable. Not only does she constantly harp on achievements in every conversation, but she also minimizes and undermines others' contributions.

Amelia is super successful, yet she has managed to alienate her colleagues because of her vanity, arrogance, and pride. Her self-important attitude has made it difficult for them to appreciate her accomplishments.

Like Amelia, are you so arrogant, proud, and smug about your success that your colleagues cannot bear to be in the same room as you? Have you become terribly lonely at the top?

Success really can go to your head—the exhilaration, headiness, the top-of-the-world feeling, and sense of extreme pride that comes from being consistently successful can all be maddening. Sometimes, success can give you a high because you find yourself surrounded by awestruck people applauding you, trying to befriend you, and, these days, following you on your socials. Once you reach those heights of success, you may end up putting yourself on a pedestal and give yourself demigod status from where you look down on everyone else as a struggler. At that very moment, you enter this delusional world of self-centeredness, which makes you believe no one is better than you: "I am perfect and undefeatable." In that fleeting moment of self-absorption, you can easily disregard and even forget everything and everyone who contributed to bringing you this far. You step into this mirage where all you see is yourself, nothing else. Welcome to the illusory world of pride!

Krishna recommends imbibing the word *adambhitvam* (BG 13.8) or pridelessness/humility—without vanity—and making it integral to our knowledge system.

BG 13.8

अमानित्वमदम्भित्वमहिंसा क्षान्तिरार्जवम् ।
आचार्योपासनं शौचं स्थैर्यमात्मविनिग्रहः ॥ ८ ॥

Amaanitvamadambhitvamahimsaa kshantiraarjavam
Aachaaryopaasanam shauchamsthairyamaatmavinigrahah

"Humility, freedom from pride, nonviolence, patience, simplicity, seeking guidance from a genuine teacher, purity, determination, and self-discipline..."

BG 16.13–15

इदमद्य मया लब्धमिमं प्राप्स्ये मनोरथम् ।
इदमस्तीदमपि मे भविष्यति पुनर्धनम् ॥ १३ ॥
असौ मया हतः शत्रुर्हनिष्ये चापरानपि ।
ईश्वरोऽहमहं भोगी सिद्धोऽहं बलवान्सुखी ॥ १४ ॥
आढ्योऽभिजनवानस्मि कोऽन्योऽस्ति सदृशो मया ।
यक्ष्ये दास्यामि मोदिष्य इत्यज्ञानविमोहिताः ॥ १५ ॥

Idamadya mayaa labdhamimam praapsye manoratham
Idamastidamapi me bhavishyati punardhanam
Asau mayaa hatah shatrurhanishye chaaparaanapi
Eeshvarohamaham bhogi siddhoham balavaansukhi
Aadhyobhijanavaanasmi konyosti sadrisho mayaa
Yakshye daasyaami modishya ityagyaanavimohitaah

"I am rich and all of this belongs to me. Tomorrow, I will gain even more. I have defeated my rivals and will overcome others too. I am supreme, flawless, powerful, and content. No one can challenge me."

If you have ever felt this way at any moment in life, you had a moment of arrogance and vanity. For some of you, this may be the natural thought process, but Krishna calls it "delusion by ignorance."

Manifestations of Arrogance (Pride, Conceit)

BG 16.4

दम्भो दर्पोऽभिमानश्च क्रोधः पारुष्यमेव च ।
अज्ञानं चाभिजातस्य पार्थ सम्पदमासुरीम् ॥ ४ ॥

Dambho darpobhimaanashcha krodhah paarushyameva cha
agyaanam chaabhijaatasya paartha sampadamaasurim[28]

"Pride, arrogance, self-importance, anger, cruelty, and ignorance are the traits of those with a destructive nature."

The root of arrogance is the sense of "doership." When "I" becomes the most prominent word in people's vocabulary, they begin to believe they are the ones "doing" everything. Check how often you use the word "I" in your conversations. That is a fair indicator of your pride and arrogance. These mostly manifest in the following ways:

1. An irresistible urge to criticize others but never yourself when things go wrong: Simply put, pride removes all goodness from others and establishes you as the one with no flaws.
2. The kind of harshness that belittles others in every situation: Such a display of arrogance goes beyond thinking ill about others and extends to vocalizing those

---

[28] *sampadam asurim* means the wealth of the bad elements in society.

thoughts in such insensitive ways that it hurts others' feelings.

3. The need to focus on appearing good rather than being good: Your pride and arrogance lead you to focus more on manipulating others' perceptions about you rather than caring about your real self or what is truly important in life.
4. The conviction that one is the sole contributor to one's success: You are too proud to acknowledge the contributions of every obvious and less obvious person or factor that led to your success.
5. Being deliberately oblivious to divine intervention and will: Many factors lead to success. One of those is divine will. Not everything is a result of human effort. When you are filled with arrogance and pride, you fail to see or acknowledge the divine element behind your achievement.
6. Hunger for attention and adulation; demanding respect: Your pride and arrogance make you crave attention and adoration, so much so that you can go to any lengths to acquire these. When you are full of yourself, you become so shameless that you force people to respect you, forgetting that attention, adulation, and respect are all earned not demanded.

BG 18.14

अधिष्ठानं तथा कर्ता करणं च पृथग्विधम् ।
विविधाश्च पृथक्चेष्टा दैवं चैवात्र पञ्चमम् ॥ १४ ॥

Adhisthaanam tathaa kartaa karanam cha prithagvidham
Vividhaashcha prithakcheshtaa daivam chaivaatra panchamam

"The five factors of action are the body (the place of action), the doer, the senses, the different forms of effort, and the Supersoul."

Five Factors of Action

Krishna lists five aspects that help you succeed in anything you do.

1. *Adhisthaanam*–the place: Choosing the right location can determine the success of your mission.
2. *Kartaa*–the doer/s: Choosing the right person or people to execute the mission determines the result.
3. *Kaaranam*–the tools: Choosing the right tools determines how you and your team will achieve results.
4. *Cheshta*–effort: Choosing to put in all effort is crucial for success. Everything—location, doers, and tools—becomes meaningless without effort. You may not achieve the intended outcome in one attempt, so it is important to put all effort into every action for the best results.
5. *Daivam*–the Supreme soul: All your efforts depend on the will of the Supreme soul. You and the others have been gifted with different capabilities to perform different actions. While you can control how to use the first

four factors, the fifth—Divine Providence—is beyond your control.

The sooner you recognize the fifth factor, the sooner you can develop *adambhitvam* or pridelessness or humility.

Arrogance deludes you into thinking you know everything; humility allows you to accept that you do not know everything. Pridefulness limits your growth by confining you within the boundaries of what you already know; pridelessness allows you to explore and grow by asking questions and seeking answers. Haughtiness locks your ability to admit your mistakes; humbleness unlocks your ability to own up to your mistakes and allows you to be human. Pretentiousness makes you hog all the spotlight by pushing everyone else out of the light because you fear your achievements will diminish; unpretentiousness allows you to share the limelight and give credit where it is due. Vanity makes you focus on your own greatness; modesty inspires you to focus on God's greatness manifesting others.

Krishna's tips for Amelia

- Recognize the pain and sorrow that comes with pridefulness.
- Study your pride to become aware of its hollowness.
- Understand your delusional ignorance to fathom the depth of your pride.
- Acknowledge the presence of the Supreme One who influences your success.

From Fear to Equanimity

Achyut has a brilliant business idea, but he is paralyzed by the fear of failure. He avoids taking steps to launch his venture. His lack of courage holds him back from facing challenges head-on. Are you an Achyut who cannot realize your potential because of fear?

Courage is not about the absence of fear but about pushing through in spite of fear. You do not know everything when you begin something new. But if you let your fear of failure freeze you even before you begin, your dreams will remain unrealized. Krishna's solution to overcoming this debilitating fear is *nityam cha sama chittatvam ishtaanishtopapattishu* or equanimity amid pleasant and unpleasant events (BG 13.10). Overcoming fear can become much easier if you can grasp this one concept well. Once you achieve even-mindedness, you will be better equipped to handle all the challenges life throws at you.

BG 13.10

असक्तिरनभिष्वङ्गः पुत्रदारगृहादिषु ।
नित्यं च समचित्तत्वमिष्टानिष्टोपपत्तिषु ॥ १० ॥

Asaktiranabhishvangah putradaaragrihaadishu
Nityam cha samachittatvamishtaanishtopapattishu

"Detachment; freedom from attachment to family, home, and material possessions; maintaining equanimity in both joy and hardship."

Life is a roller-coaster ride, with many ups and downs and twists and turns. It has elements that you desire—*ishta* and do not desire—*anishta*. It has successes and failures. In life, just as in a roller-coaster, you could go up one moment and down the next moment. So, to make your life an enjoyable experience, you need to learn to ride through the ups and downs. Some people find the roller-coaster exhilarating, yet it may not be fun for someone paranoid about these highs and lows, especially not when forced to ride on it. For them, every high and every low will feel like a death trip—an experience that may leave them traumatized for life.

Ishta represents the predictable or "known zone." Because you can predict the outcomes of this zone, you desire to remain in this comfort zone. Unfortunately, only a small part of your life is ever really in the "known zone," much of life is about simply treading the zones of extreme unpredictability or *anishta*, which represents the blind or "unknown zone." In the known zone, you are confident—sometimes even overconfident. But in the unknown zone, you are not at all confident and immobilized by fear. Overconfidence and paralysis are extreme states of mind indicating extreme arrogance and extreme fear. Krishna recommends *nityam cha sama chittatvam ishtaanishtopapattishu* or being even-minded or being in a zen state. It is an ideal state for high productivity, creativity, and effectiveness.

Aspiring for perfection is inversely proportional to fearing failure. Perfectionism hinges on the conviction that you cannot and should not fail; hence, you stop yourself from undertaking any venture with even a remote possibility of failure. Fear of failure stems from the fear of being judged by people outside and by that little voice inside your head. To avoid the shame and embarrassment that follows scrutiny and judgment by others, you could totally avoid the venture. You then tell yourself that doing nothing and not heading toward your goal means no room for failure. This thought then paralyzes you from action whenever you are in the unknown zone.

Success is not the outcome of a single herculean effort but that of improving on the thousands of failures. Every failure is feedback that tells you what to avoid. Mastery over the don'ts can make you an expert on the dos. Every successful person is a master at avoiding thousands of pitfalls learned over repeated mistakes and failures. The moment you treat failure as the end, you stop learning. But if you see failure as a learning opportunity, you become better. You can acquire this perspective only when you are equanimous or in a state of *sama chittatvam*. In a state of equanimity, you see success and failure in the same light. While success teaches you what to do, failure teaches you what not to do. Both success and failure are good teachers, you need to become a good student.

Do not feel embarrassed by failure or feel too elated by success. Instead, adopt the learner mindset of a toddler. A toddler who falls while learning to walk stands up and tries again, with no worry about anyone's judgment. Once the toddler has mastered walking, it tries to run. Every step or misstep is a learning process for the toddler. No one event is the end in itself. The toddler is fearless and does not self-limit because of others' perceptions of success and failure to walk or run. Embracing a toddler's mindset can drive away fear. It is no wonder that we learn our best lessons when we are children. As we grow older, we become increasingly cautious, and fear sets in. Children are not interested in perfection but in satisfaction.

Do not chase after perfection, chase after the satisfaction that comes by trying something new and learning something new.

Krishna advises embracing equanimity or *sama chittatvam* to be able to perceive success and failure in the same light. Being in the ideal state can help you unfreeze and achieve your desires fearlessly.

Krishna's tips for Achyut

- Seek equanimity/*sama chittatvam.*
- Develop a toddler's/learner's mindset.
- View failures as learnings.
- Ignore judgment.
- Master what not to do.

From Loneliness to Solitude

Janardhan walks through the bustling city streets, feeling lost among a sea of strangers rushing past him. He thinks he is invisible to everyone. Despite the crowds around him, he feels a painful emptiness gnawing at him. He feels that nobody cares for him. The laughter of people brushing past him only serves as a reminder of his own unhappy existence in the urban jungle. Do you feel lost too?

Janardhan was experiencing loneliness. While he was not necessarily alone and was surrounded by people, he felt lonely. Loneliness is perceiving oneself as isolated even when one craves social connections. Janardhan had friends and family, but somewhere along the way, he lost interest in connecting with people. None of them could figure out the reason for this. Unable to share his heart, he slowly drifted away from the people he was close to.

Loneliness is a modern-world epidemic that has various manifestations: an influencer who wears the façade of extreme happiness to inspire millions on Instagram with motivational thoughts but is struggling to connect with people in real life; an ever-smiling person who pretends to be the center of every party but feels lost and emotionally distant in the crowd.

Krishna suggests following *vivikta desha sevitvam* or learning to aspire to live in a solitary place (BG 13.11). Why would Krishna suggest living in solitude? In fact, it can be the real solution to overcoming loneliness.

BG 13.11

मयि चानन्ययोगेन भक्तिरव्यभिचारिणी ।
विविक्तदेशसेवित्वमरतिर्जनसंसदि ॥ ११ ॥

Mayi chaananyayogena bhaktir avyabhichaarini
Viviktadeshasevitvamaratirjanasamsadi

"Steady and pure devotion to Me; a desire to dwell in solitude; detachment from the distractions of the common populace."

Krishna recommends finding a solitary place to live so that you can become comfortable with the idea of solitude. Solitude can provide a great opportunity for "me time" to recover and resuscitate, whereas loneliness can become a punishment—something forced upon. The restless mind may confuse solitude for loneliness, breeding negativity. Krishna calls such a restless mind our greatest enemy.

BG 6.6

बन्धुरात्मात्मनस्तस्य येनात्मैवात्मना जितः ।
अनात्मनस्तु शत्रुत्वे वर्तेतात्मैव शत्रुवत् ॥ ६ ॥

Bandhuraatmaatmanastasya yenaatmaivaatmanaa jitah
Anaatmanastu shatruve vartetaatmaiva shatruvat

"For one who has mastered the mind, a calm mind becomes their greatest ally. But for one who has not, a restless mind is their worst enemy."

Imagine a small child lost in a large festival where thousands of people have gathered. How alone would the child feel even when surrounded by thousands of people? Just as a lost child feels no satisfaction despite being surrounded by people, external superficial interactions do not satisfy the restless mind.

When your restless mind meets your calm inner self, you feel the same sense of relief and happiness a child might feel on reuniting with his lost family.

Solitude gives your restless mind time and space to rediscover your true self. People who seek solitude do not feel lonely when alone or with others. Once peaceful within, they understand the potential that finding oneself holds. They also feel comfortable seeking meaningful company outside.

Your restless mind sees solitude as a dangerous thing and not as an invaluable asset, trying to frantically fill up the spaces and silences to avoid feeling lonely. In the frantic process, your mind fills up the empty inner space with readily available comforts—binge-watching, binge-eating, meaningless conversations, etc. If your mind is serene, you use your time alone for meaningful pursuits.

Loneliness feeds into the fear of being alone. So when you find yourself fearing being alone, you seek solace in relationships as a coping mechanism, often ignoring opportunities for self-discovery and growth. When you jump into relationships without inner peace, self-awareness, or connectedness with your deeper self, you experience only superficial relationships with no longevity or depth. Solitude gives you a chance to build and nurture a healthy relationship with your environment, people, situations, or God.

You will spend the most time with yourself your entire life.

Everyone else is transitory. To become worthy of your own company, capitalize on intermittent phases of solitude to focus on building new skills, developing a wholesome personality, praying, meditating, or reading thought-provoking literature. This only strengthens self-acceptance and has a cascading effect on all aspects of your life. It uplifts you emotionally, intellectually, and socially.

In Vedic culture, it was important to spend time in solitude before an important phase in life—for example, before getting married—to take time out alone to understand yourself first and then try to understand your partner.

Loneliness could also be the consequence of disappointing past experiences. Most disappointments are borne out of unmet expectations. Expectations make you hope that someone else will understand your needs, interests, and concerns. Instead of focusing on a long list of expectations, hoping others will understand and fulfill your needs, focus on understanding yourself. Solitude gives you time to understand yourself better and have rational expectations of others. When you experience loneliness, it is probably a sign that you need some solitude.

Krishna's tips for Janardhan

- Understand that loneliness is not a deathly grip.
- When you feel lonely, make time for introspection.
- Pacify the restless mind.
- Develop self-acceptance to deal with fears and expectations.
- Be prepared for the future.

From Lament to Accepting Impermanence

Anjana is struggling to accept the unexpected passing of her husband. She has been drowning in heart-wrenching grief since losing him to complications during a minor surgery. The profound sorrow of shattered dreams has left her hollow and empty. Existence has become unbearable. Are you lamenting over the loss of someone dear? Has it become difficult to move on?

Grief is extreme pain—a natural response to the loss of someone you loved deeply. The emotional suffering from grief is perhaps the most intense and overwhelming of all human emotions, causing enough pain to numb out all other feelings and disrupting life. Sometimes, it leaves the bereaved almost incapable of functioning for years on end.

Most people perceive death as the end of life, but Krishna helps us see it as another step in the cycle of life.

BG 2.27

जातस्य हि ध्रुवो मृत्युर्ध्रुवं जन्म मृतस्य च ।
तस्मादपरिहार्येऽर्थे न त्वं शोचितुमर्हसि ॥ २७ ॥

Jaatasya hi dhruvo mrityurdhruvam janma mritasya cha
Tasmaadaparihaaryerthe na tvam shochitumarhasi

"Everyone who is born is destined to die, and after death, rebirth is certain. Therefore, continue fulfilling your inevitable duties without sorrow."

In grief, pain is inevitable, but suffering is optional. Your suffering comes from your inability to cope with grief in a healthy way. While you cannot and should not ignore the pain it brings, you can only heal when you confront your grief. Crying to cope with grief is not a sign of weakness, instead it is a way of expressing your feelings about the people you loved and lost. However, pretending to be strong when you are crumbling inside to avoid confronting your feelings and expressing pain is an unhealthy way to cope with grief. Crying is not the only way to express grief; however, it is important not to store it or bury it but to find a healthy outlet for it. Death is the ultimate truth, but neither the education system nor our families teach us how to process it, comprehend it, and cope with it.

Krishna suggests gaining insight into the pain caused by the cycle of *janma-mrityu-jaraa-vyaadhi-dukkha-doshaanudarshanam* or birth, old age, disease, and death, to learn how to deal with it objectively (13.9).

BG 13.9

इन्द्रियार्थेषु वैराग्यमनहङ्कार एव च ।
जन्ममृत्युजराव्याधिदुःखदोषानुदर्शनम् ॥ ९ ॥

Indriyaartheshu vairaagyamanahankaara eva cha
Janmamrityujaraavyaadhidukkhadoshaanudarshanam

"The awareness of the cycle of birth, death, aging, and illness and its acceptance"

Krishna introduces the concept of eternity to encourage you to not look at life and death as permanent. (BG 2.27). Some stories end with a "happily ever after." This falsely makes you believe that life is eternal, which is why death comes as a rude shock. Your fantasy of "ever after" comes crashing down. Krishna reassures that death is not the period, but the comma in the story of life.

Death can make you question the depth of your relationship. What do you truly value in a person? Krishna explains that the body perishes, but the soul is eternal and passes into another body after death. So, a wise person does not lament the passing (*dhiras tatra na muhyati* BG 2.13). Krishna encourages us to value the indestructible component of the relationship that outlasts death—the soul.

BG 2.13

देहिनोऽस्मिन्यथा देहे कौमारं यौवनं जरा ।
तथा देहान्तरप्राप्तिर्धीरस्तत्र न मुह्यति ॥ १३ ॥

Dehinoasminyathaa dehe kaumaaram yauvanam jaraa
Tathaa dehaantarapraaptirdheerastatra na muhyati

"As the soul moves through stages of childhood, youth, and old age within the body, it transitions into another body at death. A wise person is not confused by this change."

Many other things last beyond death in a relationship. One of these is memories. Touching moments become etched in the deepest recesses of the heart as memories. Memories of the time spent with your loved ones last forever. You can cope with grief by re-accessing those beautiful moments with gratitude. Celebrating memories helps you celebrate your relationships.

Krishna says that the body is perishable and not worthy of lament; the soul is imperishable and not worthy of lament either. It is better to focus on experiences with the person who is no more, than lament perishing of their physical body.

Elisabeth Kübler-Ross theorized that grief has five stages—denial, anger, bargaining, depression, and acceptance.

In the first stage of denial, your mind makes a feeble attempt to deny the reality of the loss. You tell yourself that it has not happened to avoid dealing with the pain.

Then comes anger when your mind starts to process the reality. Your anger is the first outburst of emotions since you have so far been suppressing your pain in denial.

You start bargaining when you feel helpless because something you did not want has happened. You hope that it can be reversed.

But what has happened is irreversible. The reality that you cannot turn back time and everything is lost, hits you. You become sad, and this may deepen and turn into depression. You start retreating into a shell. With adequate help or self-reflection, you learn to slowly accept the unchangeable and start to accept your loss and deal with it more logically.

Understanding the wisdom of Krishna and the impermanence of life can help you reach acceptance much faster.

Krishna's tips for Anjana

- Life, death, and the soul are not permanent.
- Pain is unavoidable, but suffering is your choice.
- Memories last a lifetime; make good memories with your loved ones.
- Confront, do not avoid your grief.

From Negativity to Clean Thinking

Lavanya is surrounded by negativity at her workplace. Her colleagues always complain and gossip. Before she could realize it, she was sucked into this whirlpool, and soon found herself doing the same thing. The quality of her relationships and life began deteriorating. This change made her unhappy.

Has your outlook changed for the worse because of the company you keep?

Has your focus shifted from the positive to the negative?

Your mind has limited space. Be careful about who ends up living there rent-free. Renting it out to negative people is an unwise business plan. Most people are extra careful when considering tenants but do not exercise the same caution when allowing negative elements into their mind space.

Krishna emphasizes the word *saucham*—cleanliness (BG 13.8, see arrogance) to imply cleanliness of not just the body but also the mind, as in learning to have clean thoughts.

Shallow people have shallow thoughts. Just as a shallow pond is muddy, a shallow person's mind is muddled with dirty, toxic, negative, exploitative, selfish, and detrimental thoughts, which emit negative vibrations. Unclean thoughts manifest as negative words, which then manifest as negative actions.

Just as a deep pond is clean and clear, a person who has depth has clarity. Krishna's words and thoughts are deep and clear. Such people are genuine, empathetic, respectful, positive, trustworthy, broad-minded, and emit positive vibrations. Clean thoughts manifest as positive words, which then manifest as positive actions.

To live a higher quality of life, disconnect from shallow people and choose to associate with people who have depth in character. Well-rounded people enhance your life; shallow people diminish it.

Krishna gives an analogy to introduce the tortoise framework.

BG 2.58

यदा संहरते चायं कूर्मोऽङ्गानीव सर्वशः ।
इन्द्रियाणीन्द्रियार्थेभ्यस्तस्य प्रज्ञा प्रतिष्ठिता ॥ ५८ ॥

Yadaa samharate chaayam kurmoangaaniva sarvashah
Indriyaanindriyaarthebhyastasya pragya pratishthitaa

"Just as a tortoise retreats into its shell when in danger, one who withdraws from harmful distractions possesses a steady mind."

Recognize negativity. There will always be someone who brings negativity and toxicity. Not everyone is negative, but the presence of one toxic person can turn your entire environment into negativity.

Do not join the negativity bandwagon. Recognize negativity as it happens but also ensure that you do not contribute to it. It is easy to find faults and criticize others, but it is much more difficult to appreciate and enhance what is good. When you allow yourself to be drawn toward negativity, you join the bandwagon.

Build a thick shell of positivity around you. Just as the tortoise's thick shell is its protective mechanism, you need to build a shell of positivity to protect yourself from negative forces. Be conscious of your thoughts and keep directing them toward the positive axis. The moment you sense negativity, steer clear. Start your day with positive affirmations. Find positive friends to encourage you and support you along your journey.

Withdraw into your shell when you feel attacked by negative forces. Do not try to win against someone adamantly negative and waste your precious time and energy over something unworthy. Withdrawing into a shell is not a sign of weakness but smartness.

Relax inside your shell knowing that you have warded off negativity. Negative energy is like a bubble that bursts when it hits a strong surface. It can build up quickly, catch everyone's interest, and loom large, but it rarely lasts too long. While negativity is growing, withdraw and wait patiently for it to burst.

Resurface when you know that the negative environment has dissipated. The air will soon clear. Negative people will leave you alone when they do not receive any reaction or response from you. Rise, contribute, and appreciate others to undo the negativity they leave behind.

Tips (Tortoise Framework) for Lavanya

- Recognize negativity.
- Do not join the negativity bandwagon.

- Build a thick shell of positivity to cover yourself.
- Withdraw into that shell when you feel the attack of negative forces.
- Relax within that shell knowing very well that the attack of negativity does not last long.
- Resurface when you know that the negative environment has evaporated.

From Demotivation to Self-realization

Akinchan feels stuck because of his monotonous professional and personal routine. He feels demotivated. He recognizes the need for change, but the fear of unlearning familiar habits and adapting to new challenges has kept him in a state of inertia. He spends a lot of time doing nothing, which leaves him feeling miserable. Have you lost your motivation?

A state of demotivation is a life devoid of challenges. When life becomes monotonous, it is time to plant a new challenge because humans thrive on challenges. Aging gains pace when challenges stop.

Weren't childhood and youth life's most exciting phases? You feel that way because those were filled with challenges. You learnt something new every day and adapted to those changes. As time passes, you settle in and become too comfortable in your job or business or your home and personal life. This zone of comfort becomes restrictive, slowly eating away your ability to welcome and counter challenges and experience motivation.

Krishna suggests gaining *adhyaatma-gyaana*–self-realization or becoming aware of oneself (Bg 13.12). Self-awareness is one of the most powerful gifts you can give yourself. While it can have multiple meanings, in this context, it means becoming aware of your priorities.

BG 13.12

अध्यात्मज्ञाननित्यत्वं तत्त्वज्ञानार्थदर्शनम् ।
एतज्ज्ञानमिति प्रोक्तमज्ञानं यदतोऽन्यथा ॥ १२ ॥

Adhyaatmagyaananityatvam tattvagyaanaarthadarshanam
Etajgyaanamiti proktamagyaanam yadatoanyathaa

"Recognizing the importance of self-realization and the philosophical pursuit of the Absolute Truth—this is true knowledge. Everything beyond this is ignorance."

Lack of prioritization sets the stage for demotivation. Lack of clarity of purpose and priority can lead to an unplanned lifestyle and mindset, slowly decreasing your motivation levels till you hit the bottom. Lack of motivation can make you indulge in activities that do not need effort but give you the illusion of pleasure, throwing you into a cycle of inertia.

BG 18.48

सहजं कर्म कौन्तेय सदोषमपि न त्यजेत् ।
सर्वारम्भा हि दोषेण धूमेनाग्निरिवावृताः ॥ ४८ ॥

Sahajam karma kaunteya sadoshamapi na tyajet
Sarvaarambha hi doshena dhoomenaagnirivaavritaah

"Every effort has its imperfections, just as every fire produces smoke. Do not abandon your duties because of these flaws; instead, draw strength and purpose from them."

Inertia is the enemy of success. Even if you have the fastest sports car, if your foot is on the brake pedal, you will get nowhere. You may have the highest potential, but as long as your mind is in inertia, you will achieve nothing.

Learn, unlearn, and relearn. The moment you stop learning, you stop growing. When you stop growing, you start aging. After a certain age in life, it is important to unlearn a few things. Over time you accumulate opinions, habits, and mindsets that stunt your growth and make you rigid and inflexible. Unlearning can help you shake off your growth impediments. Once you unlearn, you can re-embark on the journey of relearning. This will bring in fresh perspectives, habits, and mindsets and keep you growing.

Krishna suggests a four-step process to take you on a journey from inertia to motivation.

Step 1–Prioritize: When you sow seeds, the first year shows no visible growth. In the second year, the plant establishes itself underground firmly but reflects no visible yield. Only after three years do you see fruit. From then on, there is no stopping its high-speed growth. Do you know why it takes so much time to manifest tasty fruit? It takes time to establish roots. The more a plant wants to grow upward and withstand all storms, the deeper it needs to reach down and strengthen its roots. When you want to be successful, your eyes are set on the sky. You often forget that reaching there needs much groundwork. You can rise higher and sustain your success only if your groundwork is strong. You can strengthen your base by finding your strengths, assessing your priorities, and charting your purpose.

Step 2–Plan: Once you know your strengths, priorities, and purpose, work through your weaknesses, faults, and shortcomings. Planning gives you clarity on what needs to be done and what needs to be avoided. It gives your priorities wings to fly.

BG 11.33

तस्मात्त्वमुत्तिष्ठ यशो लभस्व
जित्वा शत्रून्भुंक्ष्व राज्यं समृद्धम् ।
मयैवैते निहताः पूर्वमेव
निमित्तमात्रं भव सव्यसाचिन् ॥ ३३ ॥

Tasmaattvamuttishtha yasho labhasva
Jitvaa shatrunbhunkshva raajyam samriddham
Mayaivaite nihataah poorvameva
Nimittamaatram bhava savyasaachin

"Arise! Battle and reclaim your honor! Overcome your foes and enjoy a prosperous reign. I have fulfilled my role, acted as a tool, and shared in the triumph."

Step 3–Push: *Uttishtha yasho labhasva jitvaa shatrun*, that is, get up, win your glory back! Fight and win! We all need that someone (or ourselves) to push us to achieve our full potential. Everyone needs two kinds of pushes—the push from within by learning to prioritize our purpose and planning well; the push from outside, *compass roses*—people who act as a compass showing the direction, but gently. Krishna was Arjuna's compass rose. He was soft yet stern.

Step 4–Party: *Bhunkshva*—enjoy. Push yourself to the limit and then take a break. Everyone needs recovery time. In sports, pushing can help you achieve peak performance, which lasts only a few seconds but needs a hundred percent effort. Every time you reach a peak, reward yourself. Indulge in little joys. Short celebrations can enliven your senses.

Krishna's tips for Akinchan

- Reset your challenges every time you slip into a state of inertia.
- Learn, unlearn, and relearn.
- Prioritize → Plan → Push → Party.

From Greed to Simplicity

Sindhu is driven by an insatiable desire for material wealth. She constantly strives to outdo her peers. Despite her comfortable lifestyle, she craves more possessions and resorts to deceit and manipulation to acquire them. This unchecked greed has not only strained her relationships but also left her discontent and unable to find fulfillment in life.

Are you becoming obsessed with gains?

Do you assign more importance to materials and objects rather than experiences?

Are you seeking validation for what you own?

Is your all-consuming greed making you hollow?

Greed is not just hunger for money; it is hunger for anything in excess. If excessive hunger is a disease, the absence of hunger is also a problem. Having the right amount of hunger is the sign of a healthy body. Similarly, the right amount of desire is a sign of a healthy mind. *Labha* is gain, *lobha* is greed.

Everyone has desires. Getting what you desire should bring you satisfaction. But if it leads to dissatisfaction, it makes you want more, which is greed. *Labha* should not lead to *lobha*.

Krishna calls the satisfied state of mind *aarjavam*—simplicity (BG 13.12). It helps you appreciate your blessings and prevents you from becoming obsessed with and ascribing too much value to wealth, possessions, and status. Such an obsession can lead to dissatisfaction and a constant sense of inadequacy, driving you to want more to feel validated.

BG 13.12

अध्यात्मज्ञाननित्यत्वं तत्त्वज्ञानार्थदर्शनम् ।
एतज्ज्ञानमिति प्रोक्तमज्ञानं यदतोऽन्यथा ॥ १२ ॥

Adhyaatmagyaananityatvam tattvagyaanaartha darshanam
Etajgyaanamiti proktamagyaanam yadatoanyathaa

"Embracing the significance of self-realization and the philosophical quest for the Absolute Truth—this, I consider true knowledge. Anything beyond this is ignorance."

Is ambition greed? Is a moderate desire for material wealth greed? No, it is not. The desire for wealth, comfort, power, and status, when in moderation, can give you positive goals. But if you are like Sindhu and your desire is all-consuming, you cannot feel satisfied. You constantly compare yourself with others who have more. You see no end to your wants and desires. You keep wanting more and go to ruthless extents to seek validation. Sindhu misconstrued her perpetual state of dissatisfaction as ambition.

Wants → Dissatisfaction → Greed (unhealthy ambition)

Ambition can be healthy or unhealthy. Overambition is unhealthy and can lead to greed. While ambition is a sign of high self-esteem, greed is a sign of low self-esteem. Healthy and positive ambition means wanting to reach your full potential. Greed means trying to fill your hollowness with material objects. Ambition tells you "I am enough;" greed says, "I am not good enough." The constant need and greed for validation make you entitled and self-centered. Any lack of validation from others around you can make you undermine them or force them to validate you.

Kabir, a famous fifteenth-century poet, said you should use your achievements to satisfy not only your hunger but also that of others. This means that your focus in life should not only be on gaining but also giving. Developing a giving attitude can help balance your life. It will also prevent *labha* (healthy ambition or gain) from becoming *lobha* (unhealthy ambition or greed).

Krishna says that greed degrades you.

BG 16.21

त्रिविधं नरकस्येदं द्वारं नाशनमात्मनः ।
कामः क्रोधस्तथा लोभस्तस्मादेतत्त्रयं त्यजेत् ॥ २१ ॥

Trividham narakasyedam dvaaram naashanamaatmanah
Kaamah krodhastathaa lobhastasmaadetattrayam tyajet

"The three paths to self-destruction are desire, anger, and greed. Let go of all three."

Lust, anger, and greed are animalistic tendencies that erode empathy, an important human quality. Lust objectifies people. Anger degrades people. Greed exploits people. All three focus on selfish needs, interests, and concerns, all of which can make life hell. What is this hell? Hell is being stuck in this vicious cycle of wanting more to gain validation.

When you desire something desperately and do not get it,

you become angry. When you get it, you become greedy. When you do not get what you want, it is disappointing, and when you do get what you want, you crave more.

Desire is a pendulum that swings between anger and greed that keeps your mind forever disturbed.

Lust and anger have limits. Lust reduces with age; anger reduces with time. But greed is limitless because wants are endless.

Krishna's tips for Sindhu

- **Separate your needs from your wants:** Fulfill your needs compulsively but wants selectively. The mind tends to misidentify wants as needs. Discriminating needs from wants will help regulate your consumption saving you from the well of greed.
- **Collect experiences and not things:** The heart searches for deep experiences. By hoarding wealth, things, assets, cars, gadgets, properties, etc., the heart will never experience satisfaction.
- **Adopt a mindset of abundance:** Greed convinces you that you have less and must hoard more. Gratitude convinces you that you have an abundance and must share.
- **Identify the void you are trying to fill:** Greed stems from a void and the unmet need for love or respect. Can hoarding substitute love or respect?
- **Stop comparing yourself with others**: Not everyone who has a lot is happy, and not everyone who has less is sad. Seek satisfaction in what you have and what you are

and try to attain what you are capable of.

- **Beware of signs of unhealthy ambition:** Draw strong distinct lines of ethics that you do not cross under any circumstances. Recognize the need to cross lines as greed.

CONCLUSION: SHELTERED BY THE UNDEFEATED ONE

The pages you have just turned are not mere retellings of the past; they are whispers of eternity echoing through time—beckoning you to look beyond the seen and feel the unseen.

Krishna is not just a character.
He is the *composer* of destiny.
The silent architect of justice.
The smiling storm who dances through chaos, yet leaves peace in His wake.

He walks barefoot through the battlefield of the Mahabharata not as a warrior—but as the Lord of all warriors.
Not as a king—but as the King of all hearts.
Not as a mortal—but as the timeless, unconquered, and unconquerable.

To study Krishna is to awaken the soul.
To follow Krishna is to walk the path of fearless wisdom.

To take shelter in Krishna is to rise above defeat—even when the world says you have fallen.

He does not promise comfort; He offers clarity.
He does not always remove the storm; He becomes your anchor within it.
And when the night is darkest, His smile is the moonlight that reminds you—*I am here. I have always been.*

This book began as a river of stories. Let it now become an ocean of surrender.
Let your questions become prayers.
Let your admiration become devotion.
Let your understanding become *realization*—that Krishna is not someone you merely read about.
He is the Supreme Lord you return to.

He is not just the undefeated hero of an ancient epic.
He is the Undefeated within you—waiting to be remembered, embraced, and followed.

So close this book not with an end, but with a beginning.
Begin your journey of walking beside Him.
Of living by His words.
Of seeing life through the eyes of the One who sees everything.

Jai Shri Krishna!
May His grace guide your every breath, until your heart beats in perfect rhythm with His eternal flute.

ABOUT THE AUTHOR

Shubha Vilas is a lifestyle coach, storyteller and author. He studied patent law after completing his engineering degree but finally chose the path of a spiritual seeker. He has a PhD in 'Leadership Effectiveness from the Valmiki Ramayana'. In addition, he also has a Master's in Psychology and counsels people from all walks of life, connecting his understanding of modern psychology with ancient wisdom.

Ramayana: The Game of Life is his bestselling series. He is also the author of *Timeless Tales to Ignite Your Mind*, *Ancient Wisdom to Elevate Your Mind* and *5.5 Ways to a Lasting Relationship*. He has authored more than 50 thought-provoking books. The focus of his work is the application of scriptural wisdom to day-to-day life and addressing the needs of corporates and the youth through power-packed seminars.

He has delivered more than 6,500 talks, inspiring more than 7,00,000 people, across twenty countries over the last ten years. He is a popular guest speaker at prestigious universities—Stanford, Princeton and Oxford University to name a few...apart from several centers of Indian Institute of Technology (IIT) and Indian Institute of Management (IIM) in India. He has also spoken at Google, Microsoft, Amazon, Samsung at their world headquarters in USA.

To know more about him, scan the QR code

www.ingramcontent.com/pod-product-compliance
Lightning Source LLC
Chambersburg PA
CBHW062057080426
42734CB00012B/2677

* 9 7 8 9 3 4 9 3 5 8 1 7 1 *